TEACH

THE **ORDINARY PERSON'S GUIDE** TO TEACHING STUDENTS THE BIBLE

DR**ALLEN**JACKSON

FOREWORD BY DOUG FIELDS

TEACH: The Ordinary Person's Guide to Teaching Students the Bible

Student Life Bible Study
Birmingham, Alabama

Printed in the United States of America.

Student Life Bible Study
P.O. Box 36040
Birmingham, AL 35236

To order additional copies of this resource, call the publisher at 888.811.9934
or order online at www.studentlife.com

Editors: Jim Graham, Andy Blanks
Copy Editor: Kaci Hindman
Cover Design: Mike Robinson, Brandi K. Etheredge
Interior Design: Brandi K. Etheredge

ABOUT THE AUTHOR

Dr. Allen Jackson is Professor of Youth Education at the New Orleans Baptist Theological Seminary. He has the task of bending the minds of those who bend the minds of today's young people. He came to the seminary in 1994 after being in several local churches as minister to students. He is the founder and director of the Youth Ministry Institute (www.youthministryinstitute.org), an entity of the seminary.

Allen has written extensively for youth publications and has authored or co-authored six books. He has contributed to *Youthworker Journal*, *Group*, and *Leading Students* magazine.

Allen is a Texan by birth, but has also spent significant growing-up years in Georgia, Mississippi, and Louisiana. He has a business degree from the University of Southern Mississippi in accounting, a Masters of Religious Education, and a PhD from the New Orleans Baptist Theological Seminary.

Allen is the husband of one wife (Judi) and the father of two great kids (Aaron and Sarah).

A NOTE:
I have enjoyed writing this book. It is not a solo effort. The youth ministers and youth workers whom I call friends were essential in the dialog that brought this to press. Kristin Wilkerson, my assistant at the seminary read every word and made sure the documentation was in order. Jim Graham is a long time friend and colleague who edited the book. My family is all to me—Judi, Aaron, and Sarah give me an environment of love and acceptance that makes all of my creative efforts possible.

To all the youth workers on the front lines with students.

Allen Jackson
New Orleans, Louisiana
May 2008

TABLE OF CONTENTS

HOW TO USE THIS BOOK

On Your Own

The Ordinary Person's Guide for Teaching Students the Bible is a great read for anyone who loves teaching the Bible to teenagers. In each chapter, you will find **Click!** features that challenge you to respond to questions about what you are reading. The idea is for you to personally interact with me and apply what you are learning to your unique situation.

With a Group

Sit down once a week or so with a group of youth workers who are reading a chapter before each meeting. Then, use the discussion questions at the back of the book to guide a process of learning from each other. My questions will lead your group to address issues, make changes, and stay accountable as you support one another in an effort to become better Bible teachers.

FOREWORD

When Allen Jackson asked me to write a foreword for this book I was thrilled and honored. There are several reasons for my excitement, but the biggie is that I'm a huge Allen Jackson fan. Almost twenty years ago I spoke at his church and I left thinking, "He's a really good youth pastor—his volunteers love him." After he left the local church and began teaching at New Orleans Seminary, I ran into him again. I was amazed at his passion for education and for his students. I went to New Orleans to help him teach a class and I immediately became one of his students. Allen is not only a strong youth worker, he's a good thinker, a lover of Jesus, and a man with a shepherd's heart. It was with all that emotional and relational background that I eagerly jumped at the chance to read this book. I was not surprised that he delivered!

As I read, I thought of all the volunteers in the youth ministries I have served who need to read this. Youth ministry is tough! But, it gets even tougher when you're faced with one of the scariest prospects connected to ministry—teaching the Bible. The thought of having to answer questions about the Bible in front of a group of teenagers can be frightening. Don't get me wrong, those of us who lead youth ministries need adults to do things other than teaching the Bible (i.e. building relationships, introducing students to Jesus, following up, pastoral care, etc…). But teaching the Bible is a skill that must be highly valued. This book will help teachers teach better! If it's for you—congratulations that someone thought enough to get this book into your hands. If you're the leader of other leaders—congratulations for being wise enough to equip other leaders.

You might be a college student who has said yes to a summer internship. You might be a parent who agreed to teach because you are concerned about your own teenager getting a good biblical foundation. You might be a senior adult who sees that you are never too old to love students and gently guide them to Jesus. You might even be a crusty veteran of the youth ministry wars, having taught a Sunday school class for a long time. Regardless of who you are or how you got to be in a place where you might teach the Bible, you will benefit from this helpful book.

Take your time reading it. Identify with Allen as a parent or a youth worker. Think of your own stories to illustrate the solid principles you will find. Laugh at yourself and your fellow youth Bible teachers as you see your own habits in the "Top Ten Mistakes Bible Teachers Make" (page 74). I hope you will see Allen's heart the way I see it—he loves youth workers. He also loves God's Word and he's convinced that one of the ways to make an eternal difference in the life of young people is to teach the Bible in a way that is relational and creative. Now you've got the tool to help you develop and sharpen your skills.

Thanks for doing what you do!

Doug Fields
Pastor to Students: Saddleback Church
Author of *Purpose Driven Youth Ministry & Speaking to Teenagers*

Chapter 1: Who are You,
Who am I, and Why this Book?

BEFORE A WORD IS SAID about teaching the Bible (OK, except for the title), I need to remind you of who we are and who we are not. My friend Rick Morton told a story for faculty devotion (we professors need prayer too!) that bears repeating. Rick's story was about the adoption of his son, Erick, from an orphanage in Eastern Europe.

The caregivers took Erick (that wasn't his name back then, but I can't spell his original name) from his playpen and put him on the floor. Erick was undernourished, underdeveloped, and delayed in many abilities—a byproduct of being one of many babies needing instruction and attention. The orphanage worker showed Rick and Denise how Erick could almost walk, how he could eat a cookie, and how he could make baby cooing noises. Then, the caregiver looked at the Mortons for their reaction. Rick said it was if they were trying to make Erick "earn" the privilege of being a Morton by doing baby tricks.

Then Rick nailed us with a single sentence. He said, "What Erick could 'do' made no difference in our decision to adopt him into our family. We had already made the decision to adopt him, to nurture him, and to love him." That statement captures the truth of how God views you and me.

Who are you, and who am I?

You and I understand that we aren't "good enough" to lead Bible study. I am not "good enough" to write a book on leading Bible study. We aren't "good enough" to merit God's grace. Yet, in Jesus, God made the decision to adopt us, to nurture us, and to love us. God is good beyond all measure. All our undernourished, underdeveloped, and delayed abilities make no difference to God. We teach, lead, and love students because our God is good.

That is the basis on which I write, you read, and we attempt to lead youth in this incredible journey of discipleship called Bible study.

I envision that you are a youth worker, faithfully seeking to become better equipped for the ministry you have with students. I picture young adults, older adults, shy adults, bold adults, veteran teachers, first-time teachers, and people of all races, sizes, and places. (Why do I feel like Dr. Seuss all of a sudden?) I am writing to adults with various experiences, life stages, occupations, church situations, and expectations. You are the "you" of "youth ministry," an adult who cares enough to pour your life into kids.

CLICK!

Think of the names of a couple of teenagers you love. Throughout the book, think about how my ideas apply to these students.

You aren't really a "volunteer" in the sense that you have been called into this service. You may feel tired after years of ministry. Or you may feel afraid as you are just getting started. To paraphrase Joshua 1:9, "Don't bail out." You are the right person for this, and God is with you. Stop now and pray. Pray that I wrote the right things, that you will read the right things, and that God will multiply our efforts.

I love teenagers.

I am a dad. I have a son in college and a daughter in her last year of high school. I have served in some type of youth ministry for 30 years. I am a seminary professor, teaching in the area of youth ministry. I am on a teaching team in Sunday school for an incredible group of college students in New Orleans.

I am in love with a generation of youth and college students who are on a spiritual trek with me. My heart for teen-

"Though I "see through a glass darkly," I try to look through the window of the Bible to understand how to act and react, to ask and to answer, and to think and rethink. Through the pens of men, God wrote words that are worthy of being read and re-read; words that give us insight into our world and into ourselves."

agers grows when they comment on my Facebook™ page or send email, or I hear their stories from students in my classes. I deeply desire that they experience God's acceptance and forgiveness (which He explains in the Bible). I believe this generation will be changed if they associate with a community of faith and understand the God story.

I am attempting—as you probably are—to discern what God says in His Word. I want to crack the code of understanding and effectively shepherd students in the context of the local church. Thanks for joining me on the journey.

We love God's Word.

I also love to study the Bible. For me, it is no ordinary book. I like the stories, the characters, the drama, the inspiration, and the wisdom. Many discussions these days center around philosophy and worldview. A worldview is a framework or a lens through which to view life. At the risk of sounding overly simplistic, the Bible is my worldview. I admit that lots of other voices try to shape my thinking, but I try to stay committed to understand and apply biblical principles.

> If you look at a window, you see flyspecks, dust, the crack where Junior's Frisbee hit it. If you look through a window, you see the world beyond. . . Something like this is the difference between those who see the Bible as a Holy Bore and those who see it as the Word of God, which speaks out of the depths of an almost unimaginable past into the depths of ourselves.[1] —Frederick Buechner

But the kids don't know anything about the Bible.

The biblical illiteracy of the generation now in youth ministry is huge concern. Illiteracy is a big word that means students do not know the facts, the stories, or the meaning behind the stories in the Bible. They may be able to read the words, but they do not understand what the Bible means or how it all fits together.

Credible research and stories from the trenches agree that teenagers do not know the factual information of the Bible. They can't name the Ten Commandments. They don't know the difference between the feeding of the 5,000 and the feeding of the Hebrews in the desert. One survey of graduating high school seniors revealed that over 50 percent thought that Sodom and Gomorrah were husband and wife.

In *The Weekly Standard*, David Gelernter referenced the Bible Literacy Project, a study that asked, "What do high school students know about the Bible?" He noted:

"If you ask questions that are so simple the average arthropod would find them patronizing, and cast them in multiple choice format to make things even easier . . . American high school students do "okay." Almost three-quarters (72 percent) of students in the survey could answer correctly that Moses "led the Israelites out of bondage." Ninety percent could tell you that Adam and Eve were the first man and woman in Genesis. Sixty-nine percent figured out that "the Good Samaritan" was "someone who helps others." Break out the champagne!"[2]

However, the bad news is when you go a step past common knowledge.

> ". . . you find that "very few American students" have the level of Bible knowledge that high-school English teachers regard as "basic to a good education." "Almost two-thirds of teens" couldn't pick the right answer out of four choices when they were asked to identify "a quotation from the Sermon on the Mount" ("Blessed are the poor in spirit"). Two-thirds didn't know that "the Road to Damascus is where St. Paul was blinded by a vision of Christ." Fewer than a third "could correctly identify which statement about David was not true" ("David tried to kill King Saul"). And so on."[2]

Why is this a big deal? I will try not to sound like a preacher here—instead let me approach this as a dad. I want my kids to know everything they need to know to help them live a better life. When they were young, we made sure they memorized their home phone number and could call the police or ambulance. I taught my daughter how to change a tire. I helped my son with math (until about the seventh grade). My wife made sure that they knew how to wash clothes. We wanted to give them access to any information that would help them. Of course, our culture presents a lot of confusing information. So I also wanted them to know how to think critically and show discernment. If it is important for my kids to know about laundry soap and geometry, how much more do I want them to have accurate information about God, His interaction with people, and His plan for redemption?

Don't just pick on students!

Adults don't do much better. In 2000, a Barna Group study on biblical illiteracy found that three-fourths of Americans believe the Bible contains a verse that reads, "God helps those who help themselves." Other studies report, "at least 12 percent of adults believe that Joan of Arc was Noah's wife. A considerable number of respondents to one poll indicated that the Sermon on the Mount was preached by Billy Graham."[3]

CLICK!

What feelings do these facts raise in you as you think about the teenagers you love?

How ironic that the Bible is the best selling book of all time! The story of God has been preserved in ways that are nothing short of supernatural. The Word of God has not only survived, but also thrived. Benjamin Peisch, writing an opinion piece in a college newspaper described the influence of the Bible:

"The Bible has achieved its permanent bestseller status for a good reason. Charles Dickens called the New Testament "the greatest novel ever written." The King James Version of the Bible is so beautifully written that Shakespeare has been rumored to have a hand in its production—and although he probably did not, biblical references are all over his work. The Bible is the best-selling and most read book in world history. Its range of impact on Western Civilization is unmatched. . . Can Milton be understood without it? The Sistine Chapel? The Founding Fathers? The Reverend Martin Luther King, Jr.? You might even need to whip out the Bible to understand the latest Kanye West single."[4]

I believe we have compounded the problem by the way we tend to teach individual parts of the Bible without talking about the metanarrative. We've jumped from passage to passage. We've ignored much of the Old Testament. We've built Bible study around the latest "hot topic" among teens. In the process, we've missed the opportunity to help students stitch together a holistic view of the Bible.

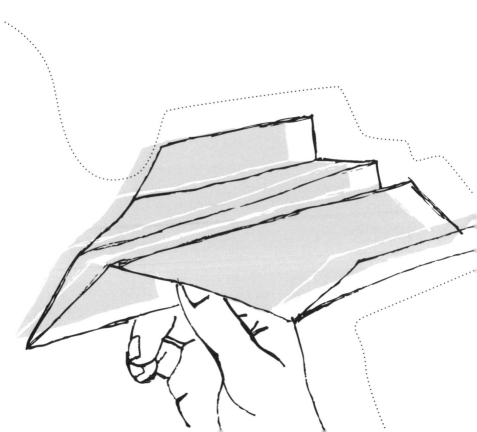

In summary, how could we not want to tell and retell the message in the Bible? If the words of Scripture guide the here and make available the hereafter, it seems silly not to try to study and comprehend. It is like needing desperately to go someplace and driving around for days to find it, only to later to learn that someone had a map and didn't think it relevant to share!

The Bible is metanarrative.

I love learning new words. The word "metanarrative" according to Wikipedia, "the free encyclopedia," is looking at things that provide a broad explanation of historical experiences or knowledge. Meta means "beyond" or "about," and narrative is a story. "Therefore, a metanarrative is a story about a story, involving and explaining 'little stories'" within the bigger story. The metanarrative of the Bible is the story of God.

The reason I bring up the Bible as metanarrative is because the students we teach have been influenced by postmodern thought. Among several aspects of postmodernism is the rejection of metanarratives. Rather than seeing a unified story, a common view of the Bible is that it is a collection of random and entertaining stories, much like Aesop's Fables. Dr. David Teague, in a wonderful article for his Web site entitled *Postmodern Preaching*, explains:

> "Like Tolstoy's War and Peace, with its many plots and subplots, the Bible contains many stories, all woven together by the one grand theme of God's self-revelation to the world. This Story of God does not come to us in the neat pack-

aging of systematic theology. It comes to us in the stories of a chosen people who experienced God. So, if someone were to ask you, "What is the Bible all about?" you could answer, "the Bible is the story of God's self-revelation to the world through a chosen people" . . . This is important for postmodern preaching because postmodernists do not believe in metanarratives. They feel that there are are no grand stories which give meaning to all of life and which define what is true."[5]

But we've fragmented the story.

I believe we have compounded the problem by the way we tend to teach individual parts of the Bible without talking about the metanarrative. We've jumped from passage to passage. We've ignored much of the Old Testament. We've built Bible study around the latest "hot topic" among teens. In the process, we've missed the opportunity to help students stitch together a holistic view of the Bible.

We can defragment the story by teaching chronologically, with the metanarrative in mind. We can help students place passages into the larger story of God. God created the world. Humanity sinned against God. God allowed Jesus to die on the cross so that sins could be forgiven. Through faith, people can go to heaven when they die. Finally, one day (in His own timetable) God will bring the world, as we know it, to a close. These are the themes that make up God's story.

I want to challenge us to reclaim the power of the Big Story. Consider the impact on Kimberly Shumate, a woman involved for many years in witchcraft. Christianity Today told her story in November of 2002 in the article, "I Was a Witch."

> "As Lisa drove me home, my mind ached as I replayed Scott's words. All the Old Testament and New Testament verses had one oddly familiar voice— one tone, one heart. I wondered, "How could a book written by so many different people over the course of hundreds of years fit together perfectly as if one amazing storyteller has written the whole thing?" The Holy Spirit began melting my vanity and arrogance with a power stronger than any hex, incantation, or spell I'd ever used. Suddenly, the blindfold I'd worn for almost 30 years was stripped away, and instantly I knew what I'd been searching for: Jesus!"[6]

CLICK!

How do you think we've added to this fragmentation?

Whether Genesis or Galatians, Exodus or Ephesians, Jonah or Joel, 1 Chronicles or 1 Timothy, the story of God's love and redemptive purpose can be seen throughout the Bible.

So what can we do?

A few years back, some of my friends and I talked about what we would like in a new Bible study plan. The language in our conversations described a metanarrative, though we really weren't aware of it at the time. The Bible study plan that came out of those discussions intentionally calls attention to the biblical metanarrative. We wanted to represent the big, historical, chronological story of God. We wanted kids to see each "little story" as part of the "big story" of God's redemptive purpose for people. We wanted students to put what they learn in context, like markers on a time line.

Tell the story.

Our first priority was to tell the big story. We wanted to capture the way God interacted with people throughout the Old Testament. We wanted to dig into the life of Jesus as the main character in God's story. And we wanted to see the essence of the New Testament Church as a community of faith.

The second thing we wanted to do was to identify the patterns or processes (also stories in themselves) that make up a bigger story. I'm not much of a symphony kind of guy (I feel more at home with the country star who shares and misspells my name). But, in a classical symphony piece I'm told there are motifs—short musical themes that are creatively repeated throughout the larger work. In fact, it is the motif that creates the unity of the piece. We wanted to highlight those themes as they appear throughout the Old and New Testaments.

Lastly, we wanted to tell the whole story. We wanted to make sure that, over time and in relevant ways, students would study every book of the Bible. Rather than choose a topic and find the verses to fit, we wanted to let the Bible speak for itself. Our experience is that the Bible will prove itself sufficient in speaking to our needs. We believe the most important topics will naturally arise from a systematic study of God's story.

"No matter how important the information is perceived to be—and no information is as valuable as biblical truth—it is best learned through relationship.

There is power in understanding the concept of metanarrative. When we study Old Testament characters, we are looking ahead to Christ. When we study the book of Hebrews, we recall the incredible faith of Old Testament characters. When we see the community of faith in Acts, we are reminded of the community of faith in Exodus. The entire Bible relies on the entire Bible to tell the entire story of God. By pulling together the threads of God's Word, we grasp what we need in order to understand and apply the Bible to our lives!

CLICK!

Take a moment to pray for the students you hope to teach in Bible study.

Live in relationships.

Before I overload you with information, I want to share the real reason why I love youth, youth workers, and youth ministry so much. No matter how important the information is perceived to be—and no information is as valuable as biblical truth—it is best learned through relationship. Relationships reinforce relevance.

I recently got a new cell phone (like almost everyone else in the world), and I decided I needed to select a cool ring tone. However, I lost interest after about a minute or two, so I had the basic "continental" tone for months. Then, my son came home from college for Christmas break. He showed me some blue-tooth hocus-pocus and, all of a sudden, my phone plays the theme song from Sports Center when it rings. As much as I love sports, I did not learn to add that ring tone on my own. I only cared to learn because it came out of my relationship with my son.

It is the same way with the Bible. This book is about good Bible study. But, like any good teaching, good Bible study involves relationships. Learning and transformation happen through relationships between youth ministers and adults, adults and students, students and youth ministers, and so on. We learn in relationships. We believe the Bible has information that is both life- and eternity-changing. Therefore, half of the equation is building relationships and the other half is sharing—as well as we possibly can—the story of God's great love and redemptive purpose for humankind.

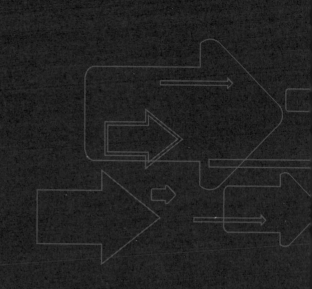

Chapter 2: Youth Ministry
as Bible Education

IF A TEENAGER SAW THE TITLE of this chapter, it would be all over. She would view it as equating youth ministry with school (sort of why a lot of folks are calling it "small group Bible study" instead of "Sunday school"). However, this book aims at teachers, who are adults.

Ordinary adults are the best teachers.

In a great book, Mark Senter proposed foundational principles for effective youth ministry. Here are summaries for a couple of key principles that apply to adult leaders[1]:

- Youth ministry begins when a Christian adult finds a passage into the student's world.
- Youth ministry happens when adults draw students into a maturing relationship with God through Jesus Christ.
- On most occasions, the influence of the student's family will exceed the influence of the youth worker.

CLICK!

Describe the most significant teacher in your church (or school) experience. What did they say or do that had the most impact on you? How can you pass that influence on to your teenagers?

Notice the influence of an adult being missional in the life of a teenager. In a healthy youth ministry, volunteer youth workers partner with parents to assist teenagers on the journey toward mature discipleship.

Think what would happen if youth workers decided to not put up with all the challenges of intervening in the lives of students. What happens if we don't try to get better at teaching and relating to youth or take advantage of technology, methodology, and even sociology? What will happen if God's Word is taken off of center stage? I might cause you to conjure up images of Jimmy Stewart in *It's a Wonderful Life*, but as adults you matter in this enterprise called youth ministry. Research suggests that these years are the last shot for reaching students with God's story. If they don't learn it now, they possibly never will.

Speaking the truth into young lives.

I tell anyone who will listen that youth workers are the most important people in the church. We get to speak truth into the lives of students! We aren't all alike (hopefully). Perhaps our differences can appeal to the differences between students. We don't teach alike, dress alike, or have the same background, ages, or experiences. What we have in common is we feel compelled to work with teenagers. This feeling is not out of duty or because we are doing penance for something we did or said at a young age. We work with youth because we feel God wants us to lead and serve with this age group.

Erin Moon, a 20-something in Birmingham, Alabama, put it this way:

> "My favorite Bible study teacher wasn't particularly cool, and wasn't 'hip to what the kids are doing' but was truly invested in my life and had a visible desire to see me fall in love with Jesus Christ. I think THAT is the most effective teaching style."

Teaching is an important task.

When Jesus spoke about leaders or teachers, He placed a premium on instruction. He knew the great Shema in Deuteronomy, which emphasizes the flow of spiritual truth and lifestyle from one generation to the next.

If we care about teenagers (and I think you do), we must learn to teach well. **We have to trust God to work,** to help us learn and develop skills, and to smooth out a few rough spots. But we also have to **invest time** learning how to be better teachers.

Hear, O Israel: The LORD our God, the LORD is one. Love the LORD your God with all your heart and with all your soul and with all your strength. These commandments that I give you today are to be upon your hearts. Impress them on your children. Talk about them when you sit at home and when you walk along the road, when you lie down and when you get up (Deut. 6:4–7).

Jesus consistently had negative things to say about two groups of people: those who were too legalistic to help others, and those who negatively affected the spiritual growth of a child. In three of the four Gospels, Jesus emphatically makes the point that children (and youth) are special in His view:

"And whoever receives one such child in My name receives Me; but whoever causes one of these little ones who believe in Me to stumble, it is better for him that a heavy millstone be hung around his neck, and to be drowned in the depth of the sea" (Matt 18:5–6, NASB; also see Mark 9:42 and Luke 17:1–2).

About 10 years ago, I went to Israel where I saw several millstones. One millstone was the size of a round dining room table, made of stone, with a hole in the center like a donut. If you had a millstone around your neck, you were going to sleep with the fishes. It sounds a little scary to hear Jesus talk that way, but it shows us how serious He is about the responsibility of teaching young people.

We need to become great educators.

Any kind of education is made up of four ingredients—teacher, learner, environment, and curriculum. Working with students in Bible study is no exception. The teacher is you, an adult (or someone who sometimes acts like an adult). The learner is the student who comes to your Bible study class or small group. The environment is the place where Bible study happens. The curriculum is the plan to teach students the Bible in context of the relationship between teacher, learner, and environment.

If we care about teenagers (and I think you do), we must learn to teach well. We have to trust God to work, to help us learn and develop skills, and to smooth out a few rough spots. But we also have to invest time learning how to be better teachers.

In a church I served in Louisiana, one of the saintly, wiser ladies used to say, "The conviction of one generation, if not communicated with passion, can easily become the preference of the next. If that happens, it is mere opinion by the third generation." From conviction to opinion in three generations! I don't want to be a teacher who causes a weak link in the chain!

Teachers who continue to learn.

Paul wrote to Timothy to "continue in what you have learned and have become convinced of, because you know those from whom you learned it" (2 Tim. 3:14). "Those" refer to the godly mother and grandmother who nurtured young Timothy's spiritual growth. From his childhood, they prepared

their young man for faith and salvation through Bible lessons (sacred writings). Paul showed Timothy the pattern of learning and teaching—passing the faith on to help the next generation "get it."

I have a confession. I do not really like to teach using activities. That isn't the way I was wired. I would rather root out the incredible content in the Bible and blast you with it. I am told, when I teach the way I am naturally inclined, it feels like trying to sip water out of a fire hydrant. Despite the fact that I am a professional teacher, I have to bend my own preferences for the sake of those I love. I must work to adapt because the mission is too important.

I feel pretty helpless in becoming a better teacher on my own. As a father, teacher, and youth worker, I don't have a prayer without prayer. We must maintain our connection with God. We need our personal time with God to pray, to bring our students before the Lord, and to meditate on Scripture. Let's carve out time to be refreshed through worship and fellowship with other youth workers and church members. Let's depend on God to do the miracle of taking our weaknesses and turning them into His strength!

It takes all of us.

I am incredibly blessed to have the opportunity to teach youth ministry students at New Orleans Seminary. I get to be around folks who will lead youth groups. Each semester, I try to convince my students that they limit the scope of their influence by trying to do it all alone. They can't teach every small group, lead every Bible study, play every game, or visit every student—at least not if the youth group is larger than about 10 or 15 kids. Life simply happens too fast for one person to be the only voice in the spiritual lives of students.

That's where you come in.

You can be an effective teacher if you will love teenagers and let that love show. Of course, you need an authentic relationship with Christ and should be willing to tell your story. Students and parents will expect you to model moral values and attitudes consistently. But, you don't have to be cool or super outgoing or play the guitar or understand video games. Teenagers don't need grown ups as peers. The best thing you can be is a caring adult willing to relate to teenagers.

You may protest that you feel inadequate to teach the Bible. That's actually pretty common. But you will be great if you recognize your limitations and do your best to work hard in study and preparation. Good curriculum materials should help you both learn and teach. Partner with an experienced team member for a couple of weeks to learn some practical skills. Pray for youth and youth workers on a regular basis. And remember an excellent response to a hard question is, "I don't know, but I will find out by next week."

Teen learners make a tough crowd.

Unlike children who seem eager to soak up anything or adults who will apply their own efforts to the learning task, students are beginning to filter information and decide whether that information will enter their brain and be recorded on the hard drive. On top of that, teenagers act like they already know

The likelihood of a biblical truth getting through to a student is related to the strength of the relationship that we have with them.

everything. Parents and youth workers wonder if teens hear anything we say.

The teenage years are possibly the toughest age to teach. We are competing for attention in a culture where information comes rapidly at the click of a mouse or remote. Think of the email that you receive on a daily basis. You delete much of it without reading it or giving it a second thought. You tend to read messages from people you know. People you know well or love much get immediate attention. It works the same way in Bible study. The likelihood of a biblical truth getting through to a student is related to the strength of the relationship that we have with them.

Teens live in their own world.
By God's design, changes occurring in the life of a teenager make teaching them a challenge. Maybe you can remember how traumatic these changes were for you. If we planned on going to a foreign country to teach, we would try to learn as much as we could about the inhabitants of that land. Though we have visited before, before we start teaching, let's get reacquainted with "Adolescent-ica."

Acknowledging individual differences, allow a stereotypical comparison:

Youth are . . .
- **Present-oriented**: Reality is "now," but the future is uncertain.
- **Daring**: Willing to take risks, but lack experience.

- **Liberal in values**: Challenge current ethics, morals, and norms.
- **Critical and restless**: Not satisfied with the status quo.
- **Idealistic and optimistic**: Driven by causes.
- **Young**: Want to be perceived as "grown up" but not "outdated."

While adults are . . .
- **Past-oriented**: Reality is based on memory and the past.
- **Cautious**: Responding to past experience.
- **Conservative**: Holding onto established manners and morals.
- **Content**: Satisfied, resigned to (and desiring) the status quo.
- **Realistic**: Cynical about life and people.
- **Mature**: Want to be perceived as "young" but "experienced."

Teenagers also tend to be rather egocentric. Not as if adults don't sing the "It's all about me" chorus from time to time, but for students it is pretty much the number one song on their play list. They love surveys, MySpace™ lists, and anything else that keeps the focus on them.

Change is the only constant.

Part of the "generation gap" has to do with the constant change in the life of a teenager compared with the relative calm in the life of an adult—at least in developmental areas. Warren Benson, a prominent writer in youth ministry and youth education wrote, "The only constant in ministry with youth is the fact of change."[2] Change can make students tough to teach because we may have forgotten the drama that comes with being an adolescent.

Change comes with growing up.

More physical changes take place during the growth spurt of puberty than in any period of life except the first year and a half. Puberty is the focal point of the early youth years. As a parent or a small group leader, the rapid changes are amazing to watch. As the body changes in puberty, the skeletal growth rate accelerates (or "launches"). Visibally, the head, feet, and hands grow most dramatically. Internally, the heart doubles in size and the lungs double in capacity. The voice changes, the genitals develop, and hair emerges in previously hairless places.

We need to make pragmatic responses to these physical changes. Youth who are bigger and stronger don't need to compete in physical activities with youth who are less developed. It may be helpful to separate boys from girls in small groups if possible. On long-term events, like camps and mission trips, younger students will not have the endurance of older teens. In contrast, as any veteran will tell you, younger teens have the corner on short-term energy. One note of caution: Don't pay more attention to pretty people and people who mature early—both types seem easier to talk to because we adults feel like we have more in common with them. Rather, build relationships with all your students.

Change involves learning to think.

The brain reaches full size in adolescence. However, the part of the brain that helps with discernment, judgment, and consequence of choices is "under construction." It may not fully develop until the mid-20s. As a result, critical thinking skills are at the forefront of what we need to allow our youth to practice.

My favorite writers who describe adolescent thinking are Jean Piaget and Howard Gardner. Piaget said humans move from concrete thinking toward abstract thinking. Children tend to think about things they can see or experience. Maturing adults think about things they can imagine. When we receive new information, we have to rearrange old information to fit in the new stuff. The fancy term for that is *accommodation*. Theology, the study of God, is pretty abstract. So teachers have to repeat, restate, and revisit theological concepts to help teenagers adapt or replace childhood notions about God.

Not everyone learns the same way. Gardner has identified a number of ways people process information. He proposed that everyone is "smart" in some way, even beyond verbal or mathematical intelligence (the traditional measurements of IQ). To describe this, he coined the term multiple intelligences. The way we learn is more than just a preference or style; it is a filter for how we process all kinds of information—math, science, sports, and even religion.[3]

Gardner suggested that there are at least eight learning-teaching approaches. I think of the eight intelligences as "personal information processing strategies."

Gardner's eight intelligences are . . .
- Verbal/Linguistic: "Word smart"—learning by writing, speaking, reading, listening.
- Logical/Mathematical: "Logic Smart"—learning by problem solving, asking questions, experimentation, debate.
- Visual/Spatial: "Picture Smart"—learning by painting, drawing, reading maps, making patterns or designs.
- Bodily/Kinesthetic: "Body Smart"—learning by dance, exercise, drama, role-play, sports.
- Musical/Rhythmic: "Music Smart"—learning by singing, listening to music, playing instruments.
- Interpersonal/Relational: "People Smart"—learning by interaction with others, working in groups, presentations, demonstrations, discussions.
- Intrapersonal/Reflective: "Self Smart"—learning by meditation, thinking deeply, goal setting, guided daydreaming.
- Natural/Biological: "Nature Smart"—learning by experiencing nature, exploring and processing outdoors, metaphors from biology and nature.

The trap in teaching is that we tend to teach how we learn. We might have to get out of our comfort zone if we really want to be effective with teenagers. For me, that means remembering to use active learning approaches. Good teachers will listen and observe (maybe even ask) so they can vary methodology to fit the learning styles of students in their group. If we spend a few minutes contemplating the normal mental changes and the ways in which individual teenagers are unique, we will become better teachers.

Change involves gaining independence.

Teenagers tend to move away from their parents for their social life sometime around the 9th grade. What they move toward are friends. This is normal, especially when the driver's license provides additional freedom. Research by the *Search Institute* in Minnesota indicates that the faith community as a social structure is critical in providing a framework for healthy transition into adulthood.[4] In other words, "Hello youth group!" The youth group is an important part of youth social life.

CLICK!

Which of these learning styles are you most drawn to? Which do you need to work on using more?

The "surprise" is that one crucial element in successfully making this transition is the youth workers who have the role of "surrogate parents." We want to be supportive adults who teens can turn to for help. While we want to equip parents to disciple their children at home, we also want to reinforce the faith students learn from their parents—and in some cases, provide what is not offered at home.

A benefit of creating the time and space for students to be together in groups is that they can practice making relational connections with other students. They can practice

"**The trap in teaching** is that we tend to teach how we learn. We might have to **get out of our comfort zone** if we really want to be effective with teenagers."

both leading and following. They can use their abilities and gifts in the context of a caring environment. As students learn to give and take in relationships in a youth group, they are better equipped for life.

CLICK!

Who is the "go to" person in your youth group when you need help for a hurting student? If you are uncertain how to answer, you may need to initiate a discussion with other youth group leaders to create a plan.

Teens feel everything.

Hormones, hormones, hormones. Rapid physical growth in puberty is triggered by hormonal changes, which mean a rollercoaster ride in metabolism (Don't you wish you could still eat like you did in high school?), sexuality, and emotions.

The mood swings that result from hormonal changes seem puzzling to parents, youth workers, school teachers—and even law enforcement. Extreme byproducts of hormone-driven mood swings include things such as eating disorders, attention deficit, self-mutilation, and even suicide. As teachers, we must keep our listening skills on "high alert" for clues that imply emotional problems. If we suspect any of these issues is a struggle for a student, we cannot keep it a secret. A simple rule of thumb is to share anything that would cause harm to the person or others. You should alert a youth pastor or other key leader of any extreme emotional behavior that you observe or have reason to suspect.

The small group setting is often a time when life issues

relating to emotional changes are unpacked. It is not uncommon for discussions (whether planned or not) to circle around love/like issues, boy-girl relationships, awareness of sexuality, or even questions about gender confusion. Students have a new capacity to care about causes—people in distress, animals in need of rescue, and communities with needs. They are emotionally vulnerable to gossip, bullying (including "cyber-bullying"), and harmful humor. The small group creates a safe environment to learn, express emotions, and love.

Teens question everything.

With the evident changes taking place in the physical, mental, social, and emotional arenas, we dare not miss the spiritual changes happening below the surface. Many students started going to church as babies. The faith of a child must mature into the faith of an adolescent and then into the faith of an adult. Decisions made as a child are often re-examined during the teen years. The whole point of youth ministry is to journey with students and their families through the important faith moments of the adolescent years.

Faith must be internalized so that it is no longer the faith of parents or significant adults, but the faith of a young adult. Only a faith that continues to develop can sustain us through life. Paul told the Philippians, "work out your salvation with fear and trembling" (Phil. 2:12). It is natural to expect that students are working on their faith as they work out the other growth areas of life.

Do not let it shock you to hear students question almost everything about their faith or the church. The goal is not to provide every answer in an attempt to convince them to see things your way. Rather, serve as a steady guide who helps them discover and possess the biblical truth for themselves.

Listen below the surface of words to discern whether the student has come to internalize his or her faith or whether is wrestling with accommodation. Trying to fit new ideas into the established understanding of childhood creates conflict that is actually part of developing a genuine faith. On the other hand, teens that are not making the faith their own may be openly resistant and express frustration at parents who "make" them come to church. Or, they may be the students who are most highly involved in the youth group, but who avoid any meaningful discussions about spiritual issues. Listen for clues to help you know how to best relate to each student's individual needs.

CLICK!

Think about where each of your students is in their spiritual growth. Use this as a starting point for prayer and conversations. Consider keeping a journal with a page for each student so you can record your observations and their prayer requests throughout the year.

The adolescent years are ripe for a commitment to Jesus. Students are open to discussions about God. As they form their identities, they often make the decision to trust Christ as their Savior. I asked Jesus into my life as a teenager. I came to church with my older sister and heard the gospel. My life and eternity changed because some adults ministered to teenagers in Bible study. They made "grace deposits" into my life as a teenager until I was ready to hear the call of God.

Create an attractive place to learn.

"Going green" or being kind to our environment is pretty much a buzzword in our day. But what is a good environment for Bible study or small group study? A good learning place is one that looks and feels comfortable to students. It may be a place in the church building, the living room of a home, or an off-site location. Choose an environment appropriate for the type of teaching you have in mind.

Remember the first impression you had when you pulled up in front of the house or apartment you were thinking of making your home? "Curb appeal" causes you to want to investigate further.[5] A good learning environment is one that looks and feels inviting. Great teaching puts youth in touch with the session visually and emotionally from the time they enter the room until the time they leave.

Some of the things that give a "thumbs up" or a "thumbs down" to the room are . . .

- **Space**: About 15 square feet per person is needed for those attending.
- **Color**: Paint or wall covering works. Clean is the real key.
- **Furniture**: Real chairs, not preschool furniture. Preferably not chairs or couches that look nasty (i.e., we don't want this in our house anymore; hey, let's give it to the youth group!). Avoid uncomfortable furniture, or items that tear clothing when sitting down or getting up (you know there's a story behind that one!).
- **Gear**: Equipment, supplies, and visual aids that attract and do not distract. Use things that are appropriate

when needed for an illustration or activity, but don't clutter up the space. Dry erase boards are almost a "must have."

- **Room set-up**: Curriculum should offer suggestions on how to arrange or rearrange in order to let the environment help you teach the lesson.

Teach the whole person.

I believe that all lessons are learned on at least one of three levels. In 1956, Benjamin Bloom headed a group of educational psychologists who developed a classification of these levels of learning. The three overlapping levels, often called "Bloom's Taxonomy," are the cognitive, psychomotor, and affective domains. The cognitive domain involves retention of information or knowledge. The affective domain includes growth in feelings or emotional areas—attitude. The psychomotor or behavioral domain encompasses manual or physical skills.

OK, I have slipped into educator's babble, so allow me to rephrase this. When you teach a Bible study to students, there is some information that they need to learn (knowledge). There is also an aspect of the lesson where students need to "buy in" to the concepts they are learning (affective). The final test of whether learning has taken place is that the lesson shows up in behavior change (psychomotor).

Consider the story of Jesus and Zacchaeus (Luke 19). Jesus was traveling through the countryside preaching the news of His Kingdom. Zacchaeus was curious, but felt like an outcast because he was a tax collector. Back then (as now) taxes were not popular. Tax collectors were considered the worst kind of folks. Jesus went to Zacchaeus' house to visit with him. In response to his interaction with Jesus, Zacchaeus repaid anyone he had wronged and chose to do right in the future.

The factual information is the cognitive knowledge to learn. The affective emotional part is that an outcast was so loved by Jesus that one conversation radically changed his life. The behavioral part of the story is to recognize that because of the conversation—and conversion—Zacchaeus acted publicly and decisively to make changes in his life. Zacchaeus reflects the "I got it" moment on all three levels. We are left with the implication that life change is possible when an outcast (like all of us) has an encounter with Jesus.

Curriculum is more than literature.

Curriculum is the sum total of everything that happens to influence learning at the cognitive, affective, and behavioral levels. The literature is only the printed materials or online lesson plan. The relationships and roles of the teacher and learners create context. We also depend on the Holy Spirit to make Bible study progress from design to understanding to (hopefully) action. That is what I mean by the statement, "Curriculum is more than literature." Curriculum is both the content and the activities that bring a lesson to life for the learner.

Everyone needs to understand the big picture of curriculum because it gives us the framework to adapt for our specific situation. Some churches utilize a team of people to teach a lesson, involving movement from a large group to small groups. Some spend the entire time with a few students sitting in a small room with a single teacher. Others meet in a living room or coffee house.

Regardless of the setting, the lesson starts in the life of the teacher before the first student enters the room. Then, it is processed in the group. Finally, it continues into the behavioral adjustments that result from the lesson (on into the week). Even the atmosphere of support from the pastor, staff, and parents is part of the curriculum.

Curriculum guides teaching.

The root of the word curriculum literally means "racecourse." The runner who wants to be successful prepares for the race, trains for the race, envisions his strategy in the race, and then reacts to the changing conditions during the race. He anticipates the challenges of the particular type of race and adjusts his pace accordingly. So, all of the elements—teachers, students, environment, and lesson content—create the conditions of the race called "learning."

There are two extremes to avoid in curriculum design if we want to get to the end and have our students really learn. At one end is the notion that the Bible is the whole curriculum. Please hear (oops—I mean read) me carefully. I absolutely embrace the Bible as essential in the curriculum process. However, the other elements bring it to life. The other extreme is to have curriculum centered on life experience and felt needs. Whatever is "hot" at the time becomes the subject of study. The Bible may get ignored or treated as an "answer book" with no regard to God's intent in its message. Neither extreme proves very useful.

Most importantly, whether the racecourse is a track or a classroom, the runner—or the teacher—must finish strong. Now that we have an idea of how the curriculum process fits together, let's look at teaching a lesson.

Chapter 3: Ingredients
of a Great Bible Study

LET'S PRETEND I'M GOING TO host a party for Helen, my favorite aunt-in-law. It is her 84th birthday, so I want to do this right. I am a bit out of my element hosting a party for a beautiful lady who is not in my generation. I want to prepare her favorite menu, but there are a few other considerations before I even get started. The ingredients that will go into the dinner will have to wait until I invite the company.

Who's coming?

The guest list sets the tone for the party. I have to anticipate who will come. Does anyone have any special needs?
It would be pretty embarrassing to serve crawfish étouffée to
someone who has a shellfish allergy.
I wouldn't want to plan a game of Ul-
timate Frisbee® if most of the guests
are from Aunt Helen's peer group. And
where will everyone sit? We all know
how traumatized you can be if you
have to sit at the "kid's table." You get
the idea. I need to think about who is
coming, how to make the experience
beneficial for everyone, and how not to let anything get in the
way of having a good time—while still achieving my goal of
serving up a great meal.

CLICK!

Describe the group
you want to reach
in Bible study. What
special needs do you
need to be aware of?

Like hosting a party, I need to think about who will be in
my Bible study so that I can appropriately plan. If I am teaching junior high kids, I may need to consider attention span. If
I know some students will attend who are not Christ-followers,
I will adjust my vocabulary to avoid "Christianese." Will it be
a large group, a small group, a girls-or-guys-only group, or a
parent group? If you are experiencing deja vu, it is because
we touched on this in the last chapter. Awareness of who will
participate is all part of the preparation process.

What's on the menu?

After inviting everyone, it is time to start planning the meal
itself. My family roots are in the South and my spiritual roots

are Southern Baptist, so that pretty well dictates that we will want to eat (a lot). When people first arrive at the party, we're going to want to have some food set out. Some folks would call it hors d'oeuvres or appetizers. We just call them snacks. The point is we want a few things out that get people thinking about eating. Then, we want to serve a main course with plenty of meat. Finally, we want a variety of desserts. Putting together a Bible study that works has a lot of parallels to a good Southern meal.

You may or may not have given input into the material you use to teach Sunday school, Bible study, or a small group. You may have material designed for a short-term study, intended for 1–4 weeks. You may have received a resource packet containing a teacher's book, or (old school here) a "quarterly" of lesson material for 12–13 weeks. Or maybe you have to come up with your own material. The point is that the materials are simply the recipes. A lot more goes into putting together a great menu than just typing up pretty recipe cards. Helping you move from the printed page to a great teaching experience is the goal of this chapter.

Bible study is a three-course meal.
Regardless of the material you are using, the teaching plan should have a pattern or a design. Think of the pattern as a three-course meal. The appetizer is to help move students toward the biblical truth of the lesson. The main course is to lead students to discover the biblical truth. The dessert is to allow students to connect the truth with their lives as they go into their world. Many labels have been given to the pattern,

"Students don't necessarily know that you, Ordinary Person Who Leads Good Bible Study, have spent much time thinking about the steps of the lesson. They may have a sense that Bible study or small group usually has a nice flow, but by design, your planning runs in background memory. If that is the case, you have hit a home run.

but for a great lesson, the parts are pretty much the same. My favorite words to describe this process are: connect, explore, and transform. I call those "the ingredients of a great Bible study."

The ingredients that make great Bible study are also found in any successful sales presentation. Whenever I think about the Connect-Explore-Transform process, I think in terms of buying a car. (Here's another confession: I worked at a car dealership a long time ago.) The connect part is when you walk on the lot and the car salesperson tries to get to know you. He or she isn't talking about cars—at least not yet. The explore part of the conversation is where you learn all the details about the car. The transform part is where the salesperson says, "Now what would keep you from buying this car today?" The goal of the sales presentation is for the customer to take the product home. If you think about it, we want students to take a lesson home, too. So, we want to put the right combination of steps together in an effective order.

Preparation is key.

Surprise! Surprise! Surprise! Students don't necessarily know that you, Ordinary Person Who Leads Good Bible Study, have spent much time thinking about the steps of the lesson. They may have a sense that Bible study or small group usually has a nice flow, but by design, your planning runs in background memory. If that is the case, you have hit a home run.

The Bible study or small group experience starts before the first student arrives. During the week prior to the lesson, the teacher's personal spiritual preparation is vital. The Bible should appear to students as an old friend of the teacher, not just a script for the class. This requires prayer, meditation, and a connection with the Scripture as a way of life. In addition, the leader should be connected to students in relationship, both in and out of the classroom. Great teachers are connected with the teaching team of adults in partnership. Finally, there is a connection with the "big picture" of how the lesson is related to the overall purpose of the youth ministry.

Connect creates an appetite.

The connect moment in the lesson plan assumes that the above connections have already been made. The next objective is to begin the lesson when the first student shows up. In a Bible study experience, we cannot assume that students are already interested in the topic of the week. The point of the connect moment is to bring students closer to the truth than they were when they entered the room. It is not the lesson—it is the bridge from culture to the text of Scripture.

Let's return to that car lot illustration for a moment. The purpose of a car dealership is to sell cars. The lot is arranged to arouse curiosity (they always park the Corvettes up front!). The salesperson understands that you are processing as you arrive. You are not sure you want attention right now. You surely don't want a bunch of brochures yet. You are not ready to talk about the value of your trade-in. So, he or she sets up a comfortable atmosphere. You may get a cup of coffee or a hot dog. Your kids get toys or a balloon. But make no

mistake—the goal is to connect you with a car that you can investigate and purchase.

The connect part of the lesson seeks to capture the attention of youth. It may be a problem to solve or a question to answer. It may be an activity to raise curiosity or a game to play. It may introduce a controversy or conflict to resolve. It may not even seem very spiritual. But every game or puzzle or drama or contest forms a bridge toward the investigation of a text and leads toward spiritual progress. From the interest generated during the connect, students are prepared to jump into God's Word.

Explore is the main course.

One of the great clichés in teaching students is, "Never teach a kid what he or she can discover on his or her own." Students are capable of and enjoy an interactive approach to learning. They are interested in the culture and context of the text. They can handle the text with integrity and honesty. The key is to let them "handle" God's Word themselves. That's not to say they are left unguided. Quite the opposite! A skillful teacher guides his or her students to discover something for themselves.

Now let's return to the car lot metaphor. The salesperson takes you straight to minivan land if you mentioned having kids (or maybe they are following right behind you). Once there, the salesperson is not the least bit concerned that your children are jumping on the seats, counting the cup holders, and finding that fold-down DVD screen. In fact, the salesperson wants your family to discover the important information about the van. He or she believes the product will sell itself.

The explore part of the lesson is when you lead students to test-drive through Scripture. Set up the environment where they "kick the tires" in Titus or they (dare I say it) take a PSpin in Psalms. Help them find the important information. Help them figure out who wrote it, where it took place, which spiritual truths are exposed, and what words or events may need to be translated for today's culture. By breaking down the key verses and putting them back together, the language of the Bible becomes the language of students.

Instead of expecting the kids to "sit still while I instill," construct the teaching time in such a way that the discovery of biblical truth seems natural. A good curriculum plan will anticipate that it is sometimes difficult to come up with creative ways to let students explore biblical truth. That is why good curriculum has so many suggestions—and hopefully one or more of the suggestions will line up with the particular learning styles of your class. Then your learners will get excited about the Bible in the way that a kid who discovers how to work the stereo in a car on the lot and says, "Dad, we have to get this car!"

Transform is the sweet stuff to take home.

When you go to the car lot, if the salesperson spends any time with you, he or she will eventually ask you to make an offer. The goal of the conversation is to sell a car. The salesperson is glad that your kids like the balloons, pleased that you asked lots of questions about the latest van, and grateful that you didn't eat your hot dog and run. You've received information, got answers to your questions, and had any mis-

Instead of expecting the kids to "sit still while I instill," construct the teaching time in such a way that the discovery of biblical truth seems natural. A good curriculum plan will anticipate that it is sometimes difficult to come up with creative ways to let students explore biblical truth. That is why good curriculum has so many suggestions—and hopefully one or more of the suggestions will line up with the particular learning styles of your class.

understandings corrected. Now it is time to pop the question: "What will it take to get you to take this car home?"

In a way, when we get to the transform section of the lesson, we also are thinking "What will it take to get you to take this lesson home?" The transform moment in the lesson is the "so what?" part where behavior change becomes the challenge. The transform aspect of the lesson is like dessert–a sweet ending that you remember as you head home. A Bible study carefully planned will be sequenced in such a way that the students have an "a-ha" moment that suggests a change in behavior, habits, or thinking. It answers the question, "What's the next step?" When a teacher sees students grasp that change is possible, they witness a supernatural part of the lesson.

Transformation is a supernatural part of the lesson because change is difficult. Psychological experts say that it takes about a month of acting differently to break a habit. It may not be instant for students (or for us) to allow their emotions to match the heart of God. It may take some time and effort for students to adjust their thinking to accommodate scriptural truth as well. This is why we must devote time to the transform process in every lesson. Students will look at our actions to see how the lesson is impacting the people of influence. Students internalize or "own" the lesson as they see direct application of biblical truth that transforms us into the image of Christ.

Set the table.

We have carefully considered who is coming to dinner (the learner). We have processed who will help us cook, serve, and clean up (the teachers). We have thought about how to make the ambience more attractive (the environment). Then, we prepared a meal with the three courses: connect, explore, and transform.

If you have a barbecue, you can serve dinner on paper plates and use plastic forks. If you invite another couple at your church over for dinner, you might use your "real" plates and everyday flatware. If you have Christmas dinner, you will probably pull out the Christmas china (you know the stuff with the ivy around the plate, just inside the gold rim?) and the fancy silverware. You serve the food on the proper plate for the occasion.

Creative teaching methods are a bit like place settings. Depending upon the intent of the lesson, you might serve it on special plates or put out different utensils. The whole presentation should be appropriate for the point you wish to make. It is possible to use creative methods for the sake of creativity (see chapter 4), and it is possible to distrust creativity entirely by preferring to "just teach the Bible" (also in chapter 4). Either extreme misses the mark.

Education folks tell us that teaching methodology can be summarized in three approaches to learning:

- **Auditory**: Information that we hear
- **Visual**: Information that we see
- **Kinesthetic (or tactile)**: Information that we learn by doing

Beyond the three teaching/learning approaches are a variety of creative methods. For example . . .

Another way to look at creative methods is to imagine where they might fit in the connect, explore, transform sequence:

Auditory	**Visual**	**Kinesthetic**
reader's theater	cartoons	role-play
dialogue	drawings	games
singing	paintings	building or
debates	photographs	constructing
interviews	murals	musical games
discussions	maps	manipulation
lectures	posters	of objects
dramatic readings	timelines	experiments
	charts	movement
	puzzles	
	worksheets	

- Connect: suspense, tension-getters, listening to records or watching videos for specific clues, newspaper headlines, varied room arrangement, debates
- Explore: reading, discussions, shared teaching, interviews, pencil-and-paper quizzes, writing a skit
- Transform: response to case studies, personal testimonies and sharing with a friend, action as a group (for example: service or mission projects)

When a teacher becomes unpredictable due to variety in teaching methods, students show up just to see what is planned. Great teaching involves learners in the teaching/learning process.

Methods are never an end to themselves, but are the means to get to the point of the text. Methods should be age-appropriate and should never cross the lines of good taste. A student who feels embarrassed because he or she was the object of a joke or got made fun of in a skit may not return. Finally, make sure that the method doesn't get in the way of the truth of the lesson. If you find it difficult to come up with something creative, consult the lesson plan. As I said before, a good curriculum plan will give you lots of creative teaching methods. The only bad method is the one that you use every week!

Clean your plate or no dessert!

In New Orleans, we love our desserts, like beignets in the French Quarter or bread pudding at a famous uptown restaurant. Before I leave the dinner party theme (How many of you had to go get a snack?), I need to ask if you have ever heard the phrase, "Clean your plate or no dessert." My guess is most of you have been a victim of parental dietary extortion. If you do not eat the stuff that tastes nasty (for me most anything green), then you do not get the stuff that tastes great (my mom's cheesecake). For some reason, our folks thought we needed balance in our diet.

Problem 1: Too much connect

The connect part of the lesson is like the salad or the hors d'oeuvres, and the meal is incomplete if that is all you serve.

Imagine a lesson where the point is that God's grace is backward from the "get what you deserve" mentality of the world. So, you contact all of the volunteers who work with you and ask them to wear their clothes backward, walk backward, and say things in reverse order. You replace the posters in your Bible study room with posters that have words written backward or the graphics reversed, or maybe you just hang everything upside down.

The kids immediately grow curious. They conclude that you have lost your mind. Youth workers aren't known for being normal, and this backward behavior explains it! However, the students decide to get into it, so they start turning their clothes around (mostly sweaters and jackets since their hats are already backward). Then, you have them hooked. Games are played that entail walking backward, talking backward, being upside down or being inside out.

All of a sudden, you realize that you are almost out of time. Quickly, you get everybody's attention and say, "Everything today is backward, and so is God's grace. It is completely opposite of the world. Let's pray." No explore, No transform, No Bible passage. . . . No real lesson.

Problem 2: Straight to explore

Explore is the entrée, but there are educational problems with jumping straight to the main thing. Imagine that you decide the text in the lesson is really intense, so you plan to go straight to explore. It might seem like a good idea if the passage is a prophetic warning that is eerily relevant. Perhaps the subject is exactly what you perceive the students in your group need to hear. Maybe the passage is so deep, so powerful, or so important that you dispense with the introductory steps and jump straight to the Bible.

The students are polite at first. The lesson flows on your agenda. Then, someone remembers something they meant to tell somebody. Another student brings up the importance of next weekend's game as a "prayer request." Still, a third student completely misunderstands the text (she thought "Job" was where you work and you were just pronouncing it wrong). The students never had a "buy-in" to the topic. No connect. No transform. Suddenly, what seemed so important to you is obviously lost on the students. Having never bought in to the experience, students end up taking nothing home. . . No real lesson.

Problem 3: Skip to transform

What if you go straight to the application? It's "relevant" and maybe "cool," and the kids will probably ask their real questions. From this perspective, the connect and explore aspects of the lesson are just a bridge to the really important part—transform. After all, what good is information if it is not put into practice?

Let's say you feel deeply concerned about the population of homeless in your town. You think the students should get involved in taking sandwiches and hygiene items to "the bridge" or "the wall" or wherever homeless youth hang out.

As students enter the room, instead of donuts, saltine crackers teach what it is like to be disappointed in the daily food allotment. You summarize an Old Testament story where God gave manna from heaven to support ("proof text") your idea that providing food is biblical. You read a New Testament story where Jesus tells us to give a cup of water in His name.

You are ready. The crackers got them thinking. The Bible made them feel guilty. You motivate the students to make some PB&J sandwiches and head downtown. The "lesson" used a weak connect, a surface explore, and jumped to transform. Like skipping to dessert, it's a quick "sugar fix" with lots of energy, but it doesn't build health. It may even make a strong memory, but without a foundation for life change. As cool as it may seem . . . No real lesson.

> **CLICK!**
>
> Think about an experience where a lesson you thought would be great never clicked with your group.

Solution: A balanced plan

The connect-explore-transform process is meant to be a three-course meal. Each course is equally important. The process requires balance. If you have a three-legged stool, if even one leg is missing or broken, it will not hold your weight. No part of the lesson is more important than the other two. It is difficult to introduce biblical text without making a connection to the teen world or experience. If the explore moment is weak or nonexistent, students may have experienced a good time, but with little or no nutrition from the Word. If you run out of time before the transform moment is suggested or discovered, students may walk away saying "so what?" (either out loud or to themselves).

CLICK!

How much time do you have to lead students through this process? What could be changed to give you more teaching time?

This stuff works.

I think my favorite story about the C-E-T process is one where all the parts were carefully planned and the lesson was incredibly effective. The man who taught 12th-grade boys in my church observed that the upcoming lesson was about a difficult subject—atonement. Atonement is the theological term that is used to describe the process by which the death of Jesus on the cross is a substitute for the price we all deserve to pay for our sins (which is death, according to Romans 6:23).

The connect moment started a week before the lesson. As they departed from the previous week, my friend instructed each young man in his class to 1) study the passage; 2) wear a short-sleeved shirt; and 3) bring some lunch money. He called them during the week to remind them of the same. The young men in his class were curious.

Connect gave way to explore as the teacher explained the third chapter of Romans. The Apostle Paul wrote about the wonderful plan of God to allow the blood shed by Jesus on the cross to substitute for the blood we deserve to shed for our sin.

But now a righteousness from God, apart from law, has been made known, to which the Law and the Prophets testify. This righteousness from God comes through faith in Jesus Christ to all who believe. There is no difference, for all have sinned and fall short of the glory of God, and are justified freely by his grace through the redemption that came by Christ Jesus. God presented him as a sacrifice of atonement, through faith in his blood. He did this to demonstrate his justice, because in his forbearance he had left the sins committed beforehand unpunished—he did it to demonstrate his justice at the present time, so as to be just and the one who justifies those who have faith in Jesus (Rom. 3:21–26).

Propitiation? Atonement? Blood sacrifice? The boys found it all a little creepy. No wonder they didn't understand it! However, the wise teacher allowed them to struggle, to talk about fairness and sacrifice and substituting for another. They understood substitution in a basketball game, but to become a martyr so another can benefit spiritually and for eternity? That's heavy stuff.

Finally, the time came to go to lunch. The teacher loaded up the class into the church van and explained, "We have a stop to make first." He drove to the hospital. The boys followed into the hospital where a man from the church was facing some serious surgery the next week. The teacher said something like, "Guys, our friend needs our help. He will lose units of blood in his surgery and we have the chance to give him some of ours." At that, the short-sleeved shirts were explained and the Bible came into better focus. The van ride to the restaurant was animated with talk of needles and bags of blood. If I remember the story correctly, at least one of the students came close to passing out.

The group arrived at the place where they would eat lunch. During the time between ordering and receiving the food, my friend asked the class, "Men, what is atonement?" A senior cleared his throat and answered, "It is like when you give blood for someone who cannot give it himself."

One of the most fascinating elements of this story is the environment in which the learning occurred. Through intentional preparation my friend facilitated the learning process in a way that seemed natural, even entertaining. And while this example is pretty complex, it worked because students came to an understanding about key biblical truths through a very simple process. You don't need to try and replicate this type of experience week-in and week-out. However, by building lessons on the connect-explore-transform model, you can consistently create meaningful learning experiences.

Send them home satisfied.

A difficult theological concept was explained through a well-crafted connect-explore-transform. The connect moment began the week before. The explore component was conducted allowing for some tension and even some unanswered questions. The transform aspect continued long after that senior class graduated from high school. The answer given by the young man was one that has helped me explain the concept almost every time I have taught the passage.

So our dinner party is a success. You (the teacher) have thought carefully about whom to invite (the learners), their likes and dislikes, even their "dietary" needs. You have carefully set the table (environment and creative teaching methods). You have welcomed your guests (connect), served them a healthy dinner (explore), and sent them on their way with a recipe for application (transform). Your students will continue to come weekly for that kind of dinner party. And, if all goes well, they should be ready to host their own party in the not-too-distant future.

Chapter 4: Ten Mistakes
Bible Teachers Make

ONE OF MY FAVORITE BOOKS on leadership is *The Top Ten Mistakes Leaders Make*, by Hans Finzel. In gentle ways, Finzel stereotypes the decisions and management styles of people in leadership positions. The book inspired me to do an Internet search of top ten mistakes. It turns out that there are lots of them. Maybe my favorite is Top Ten Mistakes Men Make While Proposing. I never realized how complicated it is to propose. I am lucky I pulled it off since I made several of the mistakes, including "proposing on a holiday or (my) birthday."

This chapter is about the top ten mistakes Bible teachers make. These are all simply my opinion. However, I asked several of my friends to contribute, so the items are a team effort. Please enjoy poking a little fun with me at all of us who have endeavored to teach youth the Bible. Many of these mistakes are common to teaching situations regardless of the content. Others are specific to teaching the Bible. I found myself in several of them; see if you can find yourself. Oh, I almost forgot . . . I do not mean to offend anyone with these. I hope laughing at ourselves can also make us examine ourselves.

Ten Mistakes Bible Teachers Make.
1. Who needs curriculum?
2. Basics are boring, doctrine is dull, and cool is better than content
3. Felt needs feeding frenzy
4. Teaching without a prayer
5. Thankful for the train
6. Text without context
7. Too much transparency
8. All activities, all the time
9. Quash the questions
10. Looking for a panacea

This book is for ordinary people who are doing the extraordinary. You are pouring God's truth into the lives of students by being in relationship with them, taking the time to pray and study, and facing any fear that you might have regarding teaching. I will try to draw some application from each "mistake" so that we can better ourselves as teachers. As a matter of fact, I think I will go ahead and change the word "mistake" to "learning opportunity."

Learning Opportunity #1: Who needs curriculum?

When we discard the notion of a lesson plan, we may be rightly motivated, but mostly misguided. I know that sounds a bit self-serving for someone who is involved in a curriculum project. There are some very good and very gifted teachers who have no need for help from preparation tools like commentaries and lesson plans. But since they are relatively rare, explore the "Who needs curriculum?" learning opportunity with me.

This opportunity offers several different variations. Some teachers say, "I'll just teach the B-I-B-L-E" (Remember the song?). This teacher may question the value of preparation tools since sometimes writers and publishers have an agenda. This is certainly true of publishers who produce a curriculum for a specific denomination. It is wise to be aware of the limitations or biases of a writer. However, it is not wise to think we have nothing to learn from another believer. Whether a scholar or layperson, we can gain some insight from someone who has studied hard to prepare a commentary or teaching plan.

The "sit still while I instill" approach where the teacher does all the talking is another version of "who needs curriculum?" Perhaps this teacher feels there is "so much to learn" that he or she must state it all as quickly as possible. As my daughter Sarah would say, "Let us talk. Bible study shouldn't

"It may seem repetitious to teach the basics of the Christian faith. What seems redundant to adults may be a first-time experience for a teenager. The basics of the Christian faith—the birth, death, resurrection, and ascension of Christ; the establishment of the Church; memorizing and meditating upon the Bible; the need for personal purity—are worth repeating."

be another hour of big church. We just sat for an hour, and we don't really need another sermon." Sarah may not be a curriculum expert, but she is 100 percent teen.

Another version of this idea is "using activities just isn't my gift." Almost every curriculum plan has activities for a teacher to use. When a lesson writer suggests teaching/learning activities (besides lecture), an attempt is made to consider various ways students learn (see chapter 2). Since most of us tend to teach the way we learn, it is helpful to let students discover truth through varied approaches.

The last version of "Who needs curriculum?" that I will mention is actually a paradox. A paradox is a condition where two contradictory things seem to be true at the same time. The two statements that make up the paradox are, "the teaching plan is inflexible," and "the Holy Spirit will tell me what to say." On the one hand is the person who sees a teaching plan as the script to be read to a group of listeners. On the other hand is the person who reads the Scripture, even meditates on it, but does not prepare any type of learning sequence. Neither works. Who needs curriculum? We all do!

Learning Opportunity #2: Basics are boring, doctrine is dull, and cool is better than content.

One of the more difficult applications when teaching youth the Bible is to remember that they do not have an adult reservoir of experience. Even a young adult who teaches a small group has more years of life experience than the average 7th–12th grader. For you as a grizzled or semi-grizzled adult

(What is it to be grizzled?), it may seem repetitious to teach the basics of the Christian faith. What seems redundant to adults may be a first-time experience for a teenager. The basics of the Christian faith—the birth, death, resurrection, and ascension of Christ; the establishment of the Church; memorizing and meditating upon the Bible; the need for personal purity—are worth repeating. Students need to hear important things more than once since they can get easily dis. . . (Did you just see that huge fly?).

One important example of the need for a "repetition principle" is the emphasis on sexual purity. *True Love Waits* is a movement among youth and youth groups to promote sexual abstinence before marriage for teenagers and college students. It is rooted in the biblical view of sexuality. A powerful youth group event is a TLW weekend. Because of the energy and expense of putting on any youth group event, it is tempting to do TLW every two or three years. After all, the students have "heard the pitch." But the incoming 7th graders have not experienced the opportunity to pledge purity. Older students have likely been exposed to new challenges in their commitment. While it may seem redundant, repetition about purity is nonetheless vital.

The same can be said for lessons that include "boring" topics like doctrine or theology. Lack of understanding of these issues is the very problem that must be addressed (see chapter 1). The repetition principle does not mean word-for-word or boring or that we focus on just a few passages. It means we continually reinforce doctrines as we discover them throughout Scripture.

Teenagers need to leave the youth ministry with a background of solid doctrinal teaching. They need to be able to speak confidently about who God is, why Jesus came, what the Holy Spirit does, and how heaven is gained. Once in college or in the workplace, the lessons students learned through repetition will give them confidence as they have conversations with persons of beliefs and backgrounds that are not biblical.

Unfortunately, we find it easier to apply repetition to issues of behavior than to the underlying beliefs. When I asked a few of my friends about typical "mistakes" that Bible teachers make, one said right away, "Every lesson eventually leads back to sex." I called it S.C.A.D., which stands for "sex, cussing, alcohol, or demons." We may mistakenly think these "hot topics" are "cool" and therefore always interesting to teens. Even with the best intentions, the pursuit of cool is so topically or behaviorally biased that we miss the truly important content.

We also have to be careful to treat the biblical text with integrity—not saying what it doesn't say or avoiding what it does say. Teachers often direct lessons to a favorite subject, whether or not the text actually addresses the topic. This mistake can be made with great intentions as a result of a life struggle or destructive experience. A wise teacher will be aware of his or her own biases and commit to teaching the full scope of the Bible.

Learning Opportunity #3:
Felt needs feeding frenzy

Have you ever heard a comedian or concert artist come on

stage and shout, "Hello, (whatever town you are in)! How's everybody doing?" It's not that they really care; it just makes for a good warm-up. The artist is playing on the "felt needs" of the audience. We want to feel special, connected, and valued. Dealing with felt needs makes a good introduction to a Bible study, but you don't want to camp there.

I am guilty of all of these mistakes (oops, I've had many opportunities to learn these) and this one is no exception. Maybe I had not planned very well or did not have confidence. Maybe it was early in the year when I did not know the students very well. Whatever the reason, it is easy to start a lesson with "What do ya'll want to talk about today?" Once the lesson is started on that note, it gets even easier to stay there. Before long, your time is up, and the Bible might not have even been opened.

I introduced you to my daughter, Sarah, a few pages back. I asked her about this as well, and she was pretty pointed. She said, "If we are just going to talk about our week, I will go hang out with someone else." She is a pretty busy girl— involved in school, church, praise team, and musical theater. Her time is precious. Many things compete with Bible study for her time. She needs to be in the Word more than she needs to talk about gossip, cliques, or breaking up with a boyfriend.

I often have found when I prepare to teach a Bible study, there are felt needs among the students that the text will naturally address. Good preparation will allow you to see a biblical perspective on the needs, prayer requests, and issues that your students are facing. In its context, you still offer wisdom

Teenagers need to leave the youth ministry with a background of solid doctrinal teaching. They need to be able to speak confidently about who God is, why Jesus came, what the Holy Spirit does, and how heaven is gained. Once in college or in the workplace, the lessons students learned through repetition will give them confidence as they have conversations with persons of beliefs and backgrounds that are not biblical.

and help from the Bible. However, to center the study around whatever the students wish to talk about that day is to miss the incredible chemistry that happens when your preparation meets God's blessing.

The Bible is not old, archaic, or irrelevant. On the contrary, while honoring biblical context and content, I think you can learn about dating from looking at everything that went wrong in Samson's first marriage (Judg. 14). Paul told the cliques of Corinthian women to get along. In fact, Paul admonished the Corinthian church on a number of issues that are relevant today:

> For I am afraid that when I come I may not find you as I want you to be, and you may not find me as you want me to be. I fear that there may be quarreling, jealousy, outbursts of anger, factions, slander, gossip, arrogance and disorder (2 Cor. 12:20).

CLICK!

What is your response to the idea that, rather than jumping from topic to topic, systematic Bible teaching will naturally address the needs of students?

Paul's reason for mentioning these behaviors was to implore the people to repent, not to have something enjoyable or "cool" to talk about in Bible study! As a matter of fact, I doubt the Corinthians wanted those subjects to come up, given their inclination to get involved in most of them.

There are many topics the Bible addresses directly. The Bible teaches many principles that can help students solve problems and navigate life issues. The main issue is to bring the Bible to the felt needs of students rather than the other way around.

Learning Opportunity #4: Teaching without a prayer

Maybe I should have listed this as number one. As adults, our schedules are packed. We try to get as much into each day as we can, often planning every minute. So when it comes time to prepare a lesson, we dive right in, sometimes going straight to the teaching plan. I must always remind myself that the first step in preparation is to pray.

I need to pray for my own understanding. I assume that God wants me to be a part of the lesson. We need time to get still and just listen. Speak to God about the things in your life that you need to bring before Him. Open your heart to what He wants you to hear. You could even remember the old acrostic to guide your prayer:

Adore God. Worship Him, as He is   merciful and He is just.

Confess sin that is in your life and ask God for forgiveness.

Thank God for His grace, His Word, and your ability and opportunity to teach students.

Supplication (intercession) for your family, friends, church, and Bible study group.

I encourage you to pray specifically for students. Pray for their families. Pray for any drama that you know about in their friendships. Pray for their openness to what God will say to them through you. The whole point of a lesson is to bring students to a point of receptivity for the biblical passage of the day. Prayer is a vital part of the connection.

Finally, pray about how this particular passage will intersect with lives. Maybe you can pray for each student according to his or her spiritual need. Pray for insight and inspiration to bring light to a passage that will be studied. Pray that you will have wisdom to hear the questions, guide the discussion, and suggest the spiritually effective changes to be made.

Having prayed for all these things, then we can study for the lesson!

Learning Opportunity #5: Thankful for the train

There are several variations of this mistake. I called this one a "mistake" because it is not really a learning opportunity. The train is the one the ill-prepared teacher prays will be blocking the road on the way to church so he or she can plan what to say at Bible study. Some people call it "red light prep" and others call it the "Saturday night special." All the labels point to the same thing—a teacher who has waited until the last minute to prepare.

I am aware that things happen that get in the way of study and preparation. Children get sick, toilets spring leaks, and soccer tournaments are scheduled for Friday night and Saturday morning. But the mistake occurs when "last minute" is the normal study strategy.

A good friend and student of mine loves to say, "Spend a week with the passage and a day with the plan." The learning opportunity comes when planning your schedule. Assuming that Bible study is on Sunday morning, begin on the previous Sunday afternoon with an overview of the next week's lesson.

Monday might be meditation on the Bible passage. Tuesday through Friday is reading the passage and commentary. That leaves Saturday to think about your plan and get the materials ready to go. Then, Sunday you will be grateful when there is no train to keep you from getting to your students.

Other things distract teachers from quality preparation. One is, "I heard a great devotion on Christian radio this week, so I will tell the students about it." "Let's just follow up on what the pastor spoke on in the early service" is another. Popular Christian books, adult Bible study groups, and current events from the newspaper—all of these compete with thoughtful and thorough preparation. Again, we want to let preparation in the Bible bring us to these cultural connections, not the other way around.

A final enemy of preparation might seem out of place here, but bear with me. When a group of adult volunteers agree to create a quality Bible study experience, the cooperation of the team is a powerful teaching method. A person refusing to be a team player, whether actively or passively, can derail the best of plans. If assignments are given and a plan is made, and everyone does their part, the Bible study experience has every chance to be effective. But if one person doesn't do his or her part, and the rest of the team scrambles to salvage the experience, the result is usually similar to red light preparation.

Learning Opportunity #6: Text without context

One of the most common mistakes Bible teachers make is to teach particular verses without considering how they fit into the rest of the immediate passage. We compound the mistake if we do not consider how the passage fits into the book or how the book fits into the Bible.

When I ask students in Bible study if they have memorized any verses, many of them can quote John 3:16 ("For God so loved the world . . .") or John 11:35 ("Jesus wept."). The last one is a favorite because it is the shortest verse in the Bible. Others can quote verses that have been in popular praise choruses or children's songs ("Seek ye first the kingdom of God . . ."), though sometimes we think choruses are Scripture when they really are not ("Like a rose, trampled on the ground . . .").

We are familiar with lots of verses, but the context in which they are found can trip us up if we don't study the entire passage. I have done this on more occasions than I can name, but one in particular stands out. I finished a study that I called, "A Deal is a Deal" and I built it around the idea that even though Joshua had been deceived into a treaty, he maintained his integrity.

> Three days after they made the treaty with the Gibeonites, the Israelites heard that they were neighbors, living near them. So the Israelites set out and on the third day came to their cities: Gibeon, Kephirah, Beeroth and Kiriath Jearim. But the Israelites did not attack them, because the leaders of the assembly had sworn an oath to them by the LORD, the God of Israel (Josh. 9:16–18).

It was a good Bible study. Afterward, I decided to look around a little in the text. The treaty was made in verses 14–

15, and my clue was the line in verse 14 where the text says that the Israelites "did not inquire of the Lord." As I did a little cross referencing, I found that God had told the leaders of the Hebrews that they were not to make any treaties with the tribes or nations in the promised land.

> Be careful not to make a treaty with those who live in the land where you are going, or they will be a snare among you (Ex. 34:12, NIV).

The same admonition is stated in Exodus 23:32, Numbers 33:55, and Deuteronomy 7:2, 20:17–18! So the point of the text was not that Joshua honored his word, but that he should not have entered into a treaty at all, especially without seeking the counsel of God.

Even with lessons that are part of a curriculum, we should ask if the direction that the lesson writer takes is faithful to the larger context. Sometimes lesson writers get caught up in the moment like I did with "A Deal is a Deal." I guess I should have called it "Deal or No Deal!"

Learning Opportunity #7: Too much transparency

The other day I learned a new term from my son, Aaron. He accused me of "Facebook stalking," which means he thinks I spy on him using his online social networking page. It hurt my feelings—I had a Facebook page before he did! What he meant was that we need boundaries on intimacy and transparency that are appropriate, based on the setting and the closeness of relationships.

Aaron and I are close. He just thought it was inappropriate for me (an adult) to constantly look at his (a teenager) profile page. For the record, I did not spy on him, though some of his friends posted a picture or two that allowed a father and son to have some "discussions."

My point is that it is tempting, in trying to relate to the struggles or temptations our students experience, to share our own story. We feel like we can be more authentic if we air out a little of our dirty laundry by telling about a time when we hurt over a dating breakup or got cut from the team. Perhaps we have a story about when we did something foolish, immature, or (maybe I'm the only one on this one) slightly illegal. Sometimes that is OK, but sometimes it is not. Let me share some guidelines that I give my seminary students:

CLICK!

What is your typical plan for lesson preparation? How might that change based on what you have read so far?

- It is never OK to share a personal story that is not true or that really belongs to someone else.
- It is OK to mention in general that we have experienced the situation, but we should avoid details and move the attention quickly off of us and back to the point of the illustration.
- It is usually better not to share our stories when asked unless we carefully consider how we will present the recollection. Even then, we might ask: "Can I make the point just as effectively in another way?"

- It is wise to consider the setting. Do you know the students well enough so that they understand what you are sharing is not something you want to glamorize? The last thing we want is for them to go home thinking, "My Bible study teacher did it; so can I!"

Similarly, we need to avoid too much transparency about current issues.

- It is never OK to let your teenagers become your accountability partners for areas in which you struggle (except maybe Scripture memory). Seek help from other adults who have victory in those areas and who have the right to hold you to your word.
- Similarly, it is never OK to let your small group become your personal therapy group. We all have hurts and grief and occasionally those make sense to share. But, it is unfair to the students and off target for the mission to make Bible study your support group.
- It is OK to share some of the on-going burdens or consequences of past mistakes. One teacher shared that he was embarrassed to visit his hometown with his family because he often ran into girls from his high school (and pre-Christian) dating experiences. Without a further detail, his class understood a very real and on-going consequence of past failure.

This generation of teenagers (and for that matter, adults as well) are interested in community, authenticity, and honesty.

The temptation is to say to yourself, "The more 'real' I can be, the more authentic I must seem." The reality is that there are times when our students need to know that we experienced the same temptations as they did. However, we cannot seem proud of our failures to the point that we glorify them. For the most part, what we need to be real about are the painful consequences we faced.

Students do not need us to be their peers; they need us to be adults. Our ability to connect with them online or through instant messenger or "texting" on cell phones is a great resource. But, without boundaries, we might blur the line between being a teacher or mentor and being another youth. It is possible to know too much about students or have them know too much about you. We want and need to exchange personal information with students, but it should remain in the context of spiritual growth and not gossip.

Learning Opportunity #7, part 2: Too much intimacy

I need to address something I wish I didn't have to write. For this one, forget what I said about a learning opportunity. This is a fatal mistake. Back in the day, we talked a lot about one-on-one ministry. The conventional advice was to try to be in the lives of students by being with them. In recent times, however, we have heard way too many stories about persons who called themselves youth ministers, youth workers, or youth volunteers, but who violated that trust.

A line of appropriateness exists between the adult and the student. Conversation needs to be fun, but not suggestive or crude. Hugs need to feel warm, but not too close or too long.

Prayer time needs to be focused on intimacy with God and not used as a platform for interpersonal relationship building. Problem-solving conversations (we used to call this counseling, but we don't any more since we are not licensed) need to be focused on the problem, not on some "you are the only one who really cares about me" dynamic.

The result of violating this trust is a trail of broken lives. No one escapes unscarred: youth workers, students, family, and church all suffer pain and disgrace. The name of God has been shamed. Some of the strongest language in the New Testament makes it pretty plain that such behavior in the community of faith is unacceptable.

Sometimes the motivation for such behavior is wickedness—a person associates with a youth ministry to be around students with the intention of an inappropriate relationship. We should become educated and enact screening processes to prevent such an occurrence. Teenagers must be protected from someone who intends to take advantage of the proximity to minors which youth ministry offers.

However, even healthy-minded leaders must remember that intimacy is a natural part of doing life-on-life in youth ministry. The upside of small group Bible study is closeness that leads to authentic discussion. The downside is that same intimacy can lead to unintended closeness, confused emotions, and attraction to students (or adults) in the group.

As we work together as a team of youth workers, let us stay on the lookout for each other. If you have a weird feeling about the apparent closeness of an adult and a student, or an adult and another adult, then pray about that feeling

"This generation of teenagers (and for that matter, adults as well) are interested in community, authenticity, and honesty. The temptation is to say to yourself, "The more 'real' I can be, the more authentic I must seem." The reality is that there are times when our students need to know that we experienced the same temptations as they did. However, we cannot seem proud of our failures to the point that we glorify them. For the most part, what we need to be real about are the painful consequences we faced."

to guard against gossip and pettiness. If you still feel that the relationship is inappropriate, go to the adult involved and prayerfully and lovingly share your impression. Someone who loses perspective should be loved and forgiven, and (with accountability) steered back to appropriate service. If the issue persists, bring it to the attention of your youth minister or pastor.

CLICK!

This is a heavy, but important issue. What are the policies or expectations your church uses to protect against this problem? For more information, see www.reducingtherisk.com.

Learning Opportunity #8:
All activities, all the time

Close your eyes and picture the students having fun. Envision how popular you will be because you never "just lecture" but instead move from one activity to the next. Celebrate the fact that your class never even has to sit still because they are always engaged in fun activities. Sounds great doesn't it? Many curriculum plans are even written with that vision in mind.

Parents probably add some pressure to this as well. Even the best parents with the most amazing Christian teenagers have battles getting their kids out of bed some Sunday mornings. Not wanting to "make" teenagers come to church, parents may subtly (or not so subtly) call for a Sunday morning approach that is "more fun" or "not so serious."

Another argument is that since you paid good money for a curriculum (either your money or the church's money), it makes sense that you would use it all. It is good financial stewardship. The logical thought would be "since they have all these activities I should use every one of them." Every activity. Every illustration. Every teaching suggestion. If this sounds a little obsessive, that's because . . . it is. And to commit to that approach would be (here's that word again) a "mistake."

Before we run out and buy something, we need to ask: "Is movement and activity the same thing as learning?" We have a bit of tension here. We have already talked about the need for variety. We have discussed the different filters that students have and how some learn better using active types of methods while others learn best with reflection. The point of the multiple suggestions for activities is that you know your students better than anyone else. You know how they learn, what kind of home environments they have, and how well your group interacts.

No good lesson writer intends for you to use all activities, all the time. Instead, select the options that work best for your group. Activities that do not accomplish that larger goal just create busy-work.

Learning Opportunity #9: Quash the questions

I searched the Web for the official term for a common phobia or fear among Bible study teachers. I came close with catagelophobia (or "the fear of being ridiculed"), but I did not find my specific phobia. So, I made one up. Let's see if you guess it:

interrogaphobia

Correctomundo. It is the fear of questions. We may fear that our questions for encouraging discussion will be met with blank stares (so we lecture). We may fear students will ask a question that will get us off track (Do all dogs go to heaven?). The most common fear—and the reason that some folks simply refuse to teach a Bible study—is that someone will ask a question for which we do not know the answer.

The antidote for interrogaphobia is exposure therapy. Ask questions, encourage questions, and prepare for possible questions. Good curriculum plans include discussion questions in the material, and these make a great place to start. If you come up with your own questions to start the conversation, try to avoid questions that students can answer with "yes," "no," or "ungh." Ask yourself, "Would I be interested in talking about the answer to this question?" And take the time to create an environment where questions are raised (by students and teachers) and answered (by both groups).

One good technique is to ask questions that contain controversy. I think the saddest verse in the Bible is:

> Samuel did not see Saul again until the day of his death; for Samuel grieved over Saul. And the LORD regretted that He had made Saul king over Israel. (1 Sam. 15:35, NASB)

If I were teaching this, I would raise questions like, What does it mean that God regretted a decision that He had made? Did He make a mistake? How is it possible that God would not know how it would turn out? I would not answer these questions. These are good questions because students will still be thinking about them when they go to bed.

A major reason not to "quash the questions" is because they serve as an indicator of spiritual growth. Most of us do not assess spiritual maturity by giving exams. I do not know anyone who was held back in Sunday school because he or she did not do well on a Bible quiz. In fact, we do not have many ways to discern if students are growing spiritually. We can watch their behavior (when they let us). We can listen to clues about their reputation. And we can listen to the kinds of questions they ask and the kind of answers they give. If

CLICK!

Is this a fear for you? How has this book helped lessened your fears?

seniors are still asking, "Did Adam have a navel?" and not, "How will I know if I am in the center of God's will?" we know there is room for improvement.

Learning Opportunity #10: Looking for a panacea

When Dorothy wanted to leave Oz and return to her farm in Kansas, all she had to do was to put on her trusty red shoes, click her heels together, and chant, "There's no place like home." When Superman wanted to bring Lois back to life, all he had to do was to fly against the rotation of the earth until it backed up a few days (Didn't that break some super-hero code?). When you want to return your abdomen to the six-pack that it was in college (or not), all you have to do is to purchase some device featured on the shopping channel and work out six minutes per day. The temptation is for us to look for an easy answer.

My friend Chuck Gartman, who has been in youth ministry for more than 35 years, suggested the biggest "learning opportunity" of all. He called this mistake "looking for a panacea."

CLICK!

Which of these 10 learning opportunities do you need to work on? Share what you have learned with your teaching team. You will help them learn and become accountable for your own application of these principles.

Gartman knows more big words than I do, so I had to go online to look up the word and make sure I understood what it means. A panacea is one thing that is viewed as a cure for everything. Like in *My Big Fat Greek Wedding* when Papa Portokalos solved every issue with, "Put Windex® on it."

We make a mistake as Bible teachers if we decide a resource, method, curriculum, or activity (usually the "best new thing") will instantly make our students perfect. It is naive to assume that any one thing is effective for all students. Yet, I have done it. I have gone to a conference or changed curriculum providers, and then been disappointed when there were not dramatic, positive results.

I do not mean to imply that changes or modifications are futile. Albert Einstein's famous definition of insanity is "doing the same thing over and over again and expecting different results."[2] It is as true in Bible study as in anything else. If we evaluate our Bible study and do not feel like we are moving toward spiritual maturity (ours or the students'), then we should try something else. And we should keep trying. But we can never assume that once we have discovered something that is popular, well received, or effective that we can fixate on that thing permanently.

Make the most of opportunities.

Hopefully by now you understand that this book has focused on the process, and not on finding the magic pill that will make everything perfect all at once. The sense of accomplishment is more likely found in the nuts and bolts of Bible study—prayer, relationships, diligent preparation, and enthusiasm about understanding the incredible story of the Bible.

These "mistakes" represent the opposite of good teaching. They are not a call for retirement or resignation. The point is to use them as a mirror in which to see yourself and improve. They may signal something that needs a major overhaul or something that you might want to tweak.

It is likely that any teacher, or potential teacher, will face all ten of these challenges. In fact, none of us are completely free from every mistake. My prayer is that we can trust God to shape us into the best teachers we can be and that we would not feel content with being less than excellent.

The dynamic components of God's story—His creative, redemptive, interactive story—are too good to explain with anything less that the absolute best of our ability. We must trust God to multiply our ability to the point where it is not simply an exchange of information, but a life-changing experience. We get to be spectators as lives are changed!

Chapter 5: What Do I Do Now?

THE LAST CHAPTER IS ALWAYS the hardest to write. I want to say enough, but not too much. So far, I have told you why I wrote this book. I am a dad and a teacher, and I feel passionate about teaching the Bible, teenagers, and those who work with teens. The Bible is metanarrative—God's story, inspired by His Holy Spirit, written by humans in a way that humans can understand. In His Word, God communicates how much He loves humans and desires that they would choose to be in relationship with Him. I wrote of the odd paradox that despite the value we Christians place on the Bible, we actually know very little of it.

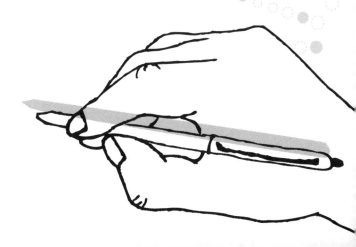

Put the pieces together.

We have talked about Bible study as education. I believe it is important that the investigation of God's Word increases knowledge about the Bible (cognitive domain), creates emotional connection to the Bible (affective domain), and changes behaviors or attitudes because of new understanding (psychomotor domain).

CLICK!

What has been the best part of this book so far?

I explained the interaction of the teacher, the learners, and the environment. Students are diverse and changing. Youth workers are vital and influential. Environments can be created to make the study of the Bible effective and fun. Curriculum is not just the printed material that we order or download, but a course of study involving everything that brings the lesson into the life of the learner. It includes literature and lesson plans, but the interaction of people is what gives Bible study life.

We looked at the ingredients of a good Bible study. Understanding the students' needs and the context of the Bible study group leads to planning. Planning begins with personal, spiritual, and prayer preparation. Anticipating the study, relational transactions with students and other youth workers on the teaching team "sets the table" (there I go again, making you hungry). The Connect-Explore-Transform language is one way to describe the three-course meal of the lesson experience.

I led us to examine ourselves and the mistakes we sometimes make as youth teachers. These mistakes can be found in teachers of all subjects, but they become crucial when the issue is teaching youth the Bible. To avoid being negative, the mistakes were labeled as "learning opportunities." They remind us that none of us have yet arrived. We continue to press on to be the best that we can be.

Be part of the momentum.

As I write, I am experiencing a previously unknown emotion. I have become a fan of the National Basketball Association. My reasons for becoming a fan have nothing to do with basketball and everything to do with relationships. I disconnected with the NBA because the way the game is played now seems so different from the basketball I almost learned (I got cut from the high school team—and rightfully so). The interpretation of certain rules, ball handling, and emphasis on star players over sportsmanship . . . well now I sound bitter. At any rate, I disconnected.

Then, the New Orleans Hornets came back from Oklahoma City, where they played while our city tried to recover from Hurricane Katrina. New Orleans is a great sports town. We are a small market, and maybe a bit of a fair weather town as far as sports teams go. When a team is winning, the energy is tremendous. When they are losing, we simply chant the mantra that has helped us with the Saints for 30 years: "Wait till next year."

The Hornets are hot this year. They not only made the playoffs, they advanced pretty far. They are the buzz (pardon the pun) of the city. Because everybody I know is talking about the Hornets, I am excited about the Hornets. I stay up late and watch playoff games. I don't have a sticker on my car, but I am thinking about getting one.

What made the difference? Why can I forgive the mutation of the game from the fundamentals that I did not learn well enough to make the team? Relationships. I enjoy sharing a passion for a team that my friends and fellow New Orleanians have adopted. People wear Hornets gear, talk Hornets talk, and act like they have been basketball fans since childhood. We "honk if you love the Hornets" and we "Fan Up" on Fridays. Relationally, we like to be part of something that has momentum.

CLICK!

What is "the buzz" in your community? Does it get more time and energy in Bible study that it should? How can you shift attention and momentum to the things of God?

Likewise, teenagers want to be part of something exciting. The good news is we have the opportunity to create the buzz, to get students excited about the church, the youth group, Bible study, and their relationship with God. The way to do that is the same as the reason I returned to the NBA: relationships. As you love your students, they will become more important to you. You will work harder to prepare for teaching. You will do more with them and more for them. And it will not be a burden, because it will happen in a relationship.

In turn, as you develop better relationships, your students will get more excited about you and the things you value. Like a jet engine winding up, the relationships will build on one another and grow in intensity. The result will be an exciting sense of spiritual and relational momentum.

Hold yourself accountable.

When we have communion at our church, there is always a time of reflection. In the Apostle Paul's instructions regarding the observation of the Lord's Supper (communion), he said:

> A man ought to examine himself before he eats of the bread and drinks of the cup. For anyone who eats and drinks without recognizing the body of the Lord eats and drinks judgment on himself (1 Cor 11:28–29).

When I am led to remember the essence of the gospel—the sacrificial death of Christ for my sins—I am instructed by the Scripture to reflect on my relationship with God. On the outside, a person can appear to be right with God while on the inside remain far from Him.

Two possibilities exist when someone is distant from God. One, the person has not begun a personal relationship with Jesus. Second, the person can be so overwhelmed with busyness that he or she becomes lukewarm to the things of God. John the evangelist described this condition:

> Yet I hold this against you: You have forsaken your first love. Remember the height from which you have fallen! Repent and do the things you did at first (Rev 2:4-5a, NIV).

When we take the opportunity to reflect, we must remember what Jesus did for us. We must worship and give thanks for the gift of eternal life through His sacrifice on the cross. We must confess things in our lives that do not honor God and take steps to deal with them one by one. I do not mean to sound preachy, but the covenant relationship with God is such a treasure that we cannot let the hectic pace of our world push Him into the background. Refer back to "Learning Opportunity #4" for a reminder on how to reconnect.

Connect to the community.

Teaching and learning the Bible in the context of a community of faith is in the genetic code of Christianity. The community of faith is the Church. Perhaps it is a Bible study class, small or large. It could be an accountability group of men or women, or a coed study group. Regardless of the makeup of the faith community, relationships within the group bring to life the story of God as revealed in the Bible. Even if you attend a very large church or enjoy teaching via some sort of media, I believe you must feel a sense of connection with the teacher in order for the lessons to "take."

If you are reading this book and you are not in an adult Bible study group, make that your first step. We cannot miss the importance of connecting with other adults. Many youth ministries have a time each week to pray, encourage one another, and study the Scripture as part of their preparation. It is essential that you, too, be fed in a community relationship.

Dig into God's Word.

Try this challenge: inventory your personal Bible study for over the last six months or so. Can you recall times that you studied the Bible either alone or in an adult group where you were not preparing to teach? If the only time you study is in preparation to be in front of a group, you miss out on an incredible blessing. Systematic study is one way to connect with God. He knows the random thoughts and abstract questions/observations that will surface in your group. When you study the Word without preparing for a specific lesson, you get ready for those questions even if you are unaware of it at the time! Here are a few suggestions for intentional personal Bible study:

Devotional Bible Study

The devotional method of Bible Study involves taking a verse or group of verses in the Bible and prayerfully meditating on it until the Holy Spirit shows you a way to apply it's truth to your own life in personal, practical, possible, and measurable ways. The goal is to become, as James 1:22 says, a doer of the Word (see Matt. 7:24–27, Ps.119:59–60).

Biographical Bible Study

This method is one of my favorites. Select a character from the Bible and research the Scriptures about that person in order to study his or her life and character. A Bible dictionary or concordance will help. You can also use a study Bible. For example, the *Life Application Bible* has character profiles throughout. Then, you can compare your own life in the light of the person under study and ask God to help you make positive character changes in your own life.

Book of the Bible Study

A book study means that you intend to get a "big picture" understanding of an entire book. The goal is to get a general understanding of the purpose, theme, structure, and content of the book. Read through it several times. Then, use dictionaries, online tools, and reference notes to discover background and context. Try to identify major characters and their interaction with God or other people. Look for a key verse, theme, pattern, or passage within the book that helps you capture life direction.

Character Quality Bible Study

Pick a character trait and investigate what the Bible says about that particular quality. A character trait does not necessarily involve specific biblical persons, though you may find people who possess the trait that interests you. Focus on how that quality can be personally incorporated in your life (or removed in the case of a negative trait).

Chapter Summary Bible Study

This works similar to a book study, except it limits the study to a particular chapter. The chapter summary is an investigation of the contents of one chapter in the Bible by reading through it at least five times, asking a series of content questions, and summarizing the central thoughts of the passage. There are "classic" chapters like Genesis 1, John 1, Romans 8, Luke 22, and Ephesians 2, which are wonderful.

Inductive Bible Study

The inductive approach involves starting from the small and moving to the large. Begin with a word or a verse and gradually expand your study to understand the key verses and concepts in the passage. The general outline for inductive Bible study is: Observation, Interpretation, and Application. Discern as much as possible from reading the text. Ask (using your own logic and outside resources), "What does it mean?" Finally, decide how the interpretation is applied in daily life.

CLICK!

Which of these methods has the most appeal to you? How can you begin to practice it in the next 48 hours? What would be the first thing you want to study?

I heard a teacher expand this outline to Observation, Interpretation, Implication, Application. The added step takes "What does it mean?" and adds, "What does it mean in my life right now?"

Topical Bible Study

A topical Bible study involves selecting a subject of interest (such as anger, love, speech, or friendship) and tracing it throughout a single book, the Old or New Testament, or the entire Bible. A concordance will be extremely helpful. There are many good research tools online as well.

Practice what you have learned.

Since we are on the topic of topics, let's do a topical study together. I am interested in what the Bible says about the role of a teacher. I begin my search using a free online tool found at www.gospelgateway.com. I click on "Topical Index," and searched the Nave's Topical Bible (also available in print), which suggested 40 references. Using a concordance, I find 55 references for "teacher" in the New Testament alone. I have plenty of verses to look up to gain understanding.

A quick glance shows that some of the references are not relevant to a study of the role of a teacher. One category that is extremely relevant is that of authenticity. Several verses refer to "false teachers" and since I do not want to mislead anyone, especially teenagers, I am paying attention. Among the verses are:

Am I now trying to win the approval of men, or of God? Or am I trying to please men? If I were still trying to please men, I would not be a servant of Christ (Gal. 1:10).

Those people [who belong to the circumcision group] are zealous to win you over, but for no good. What they want is to alienate you from us, so that you may be zealous for them (Gal. 4:17).

They are the kind who worm their way into homes and gain control over weak-willed women, who are loaded down with sins and are swayed by all kinds of evil desires (2 Tim. 3:6).

In their greed these teachers will exploit you with stories they have made up. Their condemnation has long been hanging over them, and their destruction has not been sleeping (2 Pet. 2:3).

In these verses we find:

- Spiritual teachers seek to please God and not people
- Just because teachers are likeable and convincing does not mean that they speak the truth
- Wrongly motivated teachers take advantage of people who have problems and are looking for relief
- Some teachers who claim to be spiritual embellish or replace the truth with their own stories

The Bible speaks about the teacher's humility, influence, work ethic, and responsibility. Matthew wrote, "Nor are you to be called 'teacher,' for you have one Teacher, the Christ. The greatest among you will be your servant. For whoever exalts himself will be humbled, and whoever humbles himself will be exalted" (Matt. 23:10–12). Humility does not mean we are without influence. "A student is not above his teacher, nor a servant above his master. It is enough for the student to be like his teacher, and the servant like his master" (Matt. 10:24–25a). James warns that the high responsibility of the teacher demands a strong work ethic:

Don't be in any rush to become a teacher, my friends. Teaching is highly responsible work. Teachers are held to the strictest standards. And none of us is perfectly qualified. We get it wrong nearly every time we open our mouths. If you could find someone whose speech was perfectly true, you'd have a perfect person, in perfect control of life (Jas. 3:1–2, MSG).

Without looking at all of the verses that deal with the role of teachers, we can see a pattern. The incredible privilege of teaching the Bible to students comes with great responsibility. Before you get discouraged or feel as if you are not up to the task, look at one more verse. God chose us as teachers:

It was he who gave some to be apostles, some to be prophets, some to be evangelists, and some to be pastors and teachers, to prepare God's people for works of service, so that the body of Christ may be built up until we all reach unity in the faith and in the knowledge of the Son of God and become mature, attaining to the whole measure of the fullness of Christ (Eph. 4:11–13).

If you have made it this far in this book, I think it is fair to assume that you sense a calling to be a teacher. God put it there! His reason for calling you is so you can prepare your students for works of service for the Lord. You are able to encourage them in their faith and help them increase in knowledge of the Bible. This partnership with God means that He calls you to teach and you trust Him to help you be a good teacher. The result is that students are maturing to become more like Christ.

Customize your teaching plan.

One of the signature plays used by the 2008 Hornets is the alley-oop where Chris Paul (the point guard) lobs a pass just above the rim for Tyson Chandler (a big guy by the basket). Chandler grabs the pass and slams it through the goal for a relatively high-percentage two-point bucket. When Paul starts that pass, he is sure (most of the time) that Chandler is there. If the Hornets need a three-point play, Paul will drive and then kick a pass away from the basket to Peja Stojak-ovic (that drove my spell check crazy). My point is that the pass depends on the receiver.

CLICK!

How do you feel about the responsibility you have in teaching? How does God's call on your life and the way He has gifted you play into how you feel?

Each student and each small group is different. Different "receivers" require different approaches. Remember, an approach or learning style is the way a learner prefers to gather and process information. Learning styles include the human ability to understand truth, both concrete and abstract. This ability grows out of the individual's physical, emotional, social, mental, and spiritual development (chapter 2). Remember that younger youth are moving intellectually from concrete thinking to abstract (conceptual) thinking. The wise teacher considers the youth's intellectual development when selecting a teaching method.

Although every person has a dominant approach to learning, everyone can learn through a combination of several approaches. The connection is that in each of the three parts of the teaching/learning experience—connect, explore, transform—a teacher can choose an activity that aims toward one or more of the approaches. Students will be drawn to lessons that speak to their preferred learning style. A good conversation with your group might be to show them the eight intelligences (chapter 2) and ask them which one or two they think describes them best. Then, you have a fun place to start when you begin preparation for your next lesson!

Chose great materials.

As a youth worker and youth educator, use the information you have gleaned to look at youth ministry resources. Take a look at Bible study materials. Play with online curriculum. Review some video-based studies. Revisit things you have passed on before to see if they don't make better sense now that you have a better understanding of the preparation and teaching process.

Whatever resource you handle, it is a good idea to be aware of the doctrinal position of the company that produces the resources. Any reputable resource provider should have a doctrinal statement. Be aware of any biases that the resource provider might have due to denominational ties.

Sample resources to see what best fits the needs and style of your group. Be a team player—let your voice combine with other voices in your youth ministry to choose a curriculum plan that is compatible with your group size, your budget, and your specific setting. The material should be simple enough to understand, but complex (deep) enough to challenge students. It should be affordable, but not cheap or cheesy in its actual content. Good curriculum is usually expensive to develop. If you get something that is free, beware—often you get what you pay for!

Make sure that the resources you choose are flexible. Teaching plans should address various "intelligences," age ranges, groupings and teaching formats (master teacher or small group). There should be multiple suggestions for each stage of the lesson so that you as a teacher can prayerfully select the best sequence for your group. You know them best and love them most!

Build a shop full of tools.

If you have ever worked on a car or done a project around the house, you know the value of the right tools. More than once, I have been in the middle of a job, with grease up to my elbows or ankle deep in dirt only to discover that I did not have what I needed. I would have to clean up, spread a towel over the seat in the car, and go to the store. The time spent trying to find the right tools often means I end up running out of time to do my original project.

I recommend that you start now to stock your Bible study reference toolbox. Begin to build a library. Talk to your pastor or other veteran teachers about commentary sets, Bible dictionaries, or word study resources. Locate online tools that are helpful. You might find it useful to purchase a Bible study program for your computer. Bible encyclopedias will assist with chronology, timelines, and cultural context for a lesson. Your own library will make study very efficient because you will have all of the tools in one place.

Remember the relationships.

As you study, you should visualize the students you will teach. Constantly work on relationships. When you have a genuine relationship with a teenager, you are more likely to receive a positive response in Bible study. If youth trust that you care about them and have their best interest in mind, they are more likely to follow your leadership, even if you have to provide loving discipline.

Seek to understand individual youth. Sometimes we expect that the kids in our class will be just like the kids from last year. Or we may compare one youth with another in our class. With the volatile nature of the adolescent years, it may not even be reasonable to compare a student today with the same student yesterday!

Let youth be young. Teens are noisy, active, and easily distracted. Expecting youth to behave as adults is expecting the impossible. Controlled chaos may be a more accurate description of youth's learning experiences than a quiet, orderly situation (that probably exists only in dreams).

Be a mentor.

If you are just starting out, find a veteran teacher to observe. Pick his or her brain about resources, preparation, and planning. Ask about crowd control. Listen to stories about transformation that happened when a student made a discovery that changed the student's life. Become an apprentice to a veteran teacher, team teaching for a year or so. You may learn many healthy shortcuts from watching and seeing how an experienced teacher handles challenges.

Likewise, if you are a veteran teacher, look for a potential teacher to take under your wing. Buy them a copy of this book and go through it with them. Allow them to lead some activities in your group as they learn about teaching. At some point, when your group has grown or when another teaching position is open, your youth ministry will benefit from a person who has been prepared to teach.

Shine your light.

All of us are needed in this effort called youth ministry. Parents need to learn how to disciple their children and take that role seriously. Youth teachers need to work with families to create a culture where the Bible is seen as valuable, authoritative, and inspired. Pastors and church leaders need to recognize that God has called them to be a moral and spiritual voice in the community. Each member of the church needs to prepare to assume a teaching or serving role as needs become known. This fable illustrates the point:

> In a certain mountain village in Europe several centuries ago, a nobleman wondered what legacy he should leave to his townspeople. At last he decided to build them a church. No one saw the complete plans for the church until it was finished. When the people gathered, they marveled at its beauty and completeness. Then someone asked, "But where are the lamps? How will it be lighted?" The nobleman pointed to some brackets in the walls. Then he gave to each family a lamp, which they were to bring with them each time they came to worship. "Each time you are here the area

where you are seated will be lighted," the nobleman said. "Each time you are not here, that area will be dark. This is to remind you that whenever you fail to come to church, some part of God's house will be dark."

CLICK!

Who could you enlist to come alongside of you so they are prepared to be a youth Bible study teacher?

I have faith in a generation of youth Bible study leaders—ordinary as you consider yourself—who will do extraordinary things because you allow God to use you. I have faith that a few committed students will rise up in every community and in every church to become the prophetic voice needed in this culture. It just might be that one of these days, a student or two will come find you and thank you for the difference that you made in their lives. Thanks for joining me on this journey.

GROUP DISCUSSION QUESTIONS

Chapter 1:

1. Share with the group why you are a youth Bible Study leader.
2. Discuss your thoughts about the biblical literacy of the students in your youth group. How would you say they compare to the research?
3. Student Life Bible Study is a multi-year plan to improve your student's Bible knowledge and application. What needs to be done for such a plan to fit into your church's direction for youth ministry?
4. What about the content of this chapter excites you as a leader?

Chapter 2:

1. Discuss the expectations for youth workers in your church in the areas of teaching, relationship building, and participation in youth events.
2. "Curriculum is a racecourse." Share your thoughts on what you see as the "finish line" of your teaching ministry, the goals or outcomes you hope to see in students.
3. Set some group goals for improvements in ministry effectiveness for the coming 6 to 12 months.
4. As you evaluate this chapter, what elements have stood out as things you personally need to work on?

Chapter 3:

1. Tell about a time when a lesson really clicked with your group or a time one really bombed.

2. Discuss ways you can use more variety of teaching methods in the Bible study experience.
3. Make a shopping list of supplies and resources you need to gather to be ready to use more creative teaching methods.
4. Create a plan for maximizing the entire Bible study time so there is a priority on leading a great learning experience.

Chapter 4:

1. Which of the "mistakes" was most insightful to you?
2. If your team worked to make great improvements in just one of these learning opportunities, which do you feel would be most effective at helping students know the Word? Decide on one or two that everyone agrees to work on.
3. Discuss your church's policies or expectations for maintaining proper adult-to-student relationships. If none exist, decide how to take the first steps to develop some guidelines.
4. Spend time praying together for the effectiveness of your teaching team and the spiritual growth of students.

Chapter 5:

1. What is your best "take away" from this book?
2. What are your personal goals for your own spiritual growth? For your development as a teacher?
3. How can your team of leaders support one another as you take on the important task of teaching students God's Word?
4. Schedule a time in three to six months for your team to regroup and review your progress as you seek to become better teachers and spiritual leaders.

End Notes

Chapter 1

1. Frederick Buechner, *Wishful Thinking* (New York: Harper Collins Publishers, 1973), 12.
2. David Gelernter, "Bible Illiteracy in America," *The Weekly Standard* (Volume 010, Issue 34), May 23, 2005.
3. Barna Group, see a number of studies investigating comprehension and knowledge of Bible truth. Found at http://www.barna.org, accessed April 2008.
4. Benjamin Peisch, "Bible deserves place in world of academia," *The Bowdoin Orient: newspaper of Bowdoin College*, Brunswick, Maine, February 4, 2005. Found at http://orient.bowdoin.edu/orient, accessed April 2008.
5. David Teague, "The biblical narrative," http://www.postmodernpreaching.net, accessed February 2008.
6. Kimberly Shumate, "I Was a Witch", *Today's Christian Woman*, http://www.christianitytoday.com/tcw/2002/sepoct/20.38.html, accessed May 2008.

Chapter 2

1. Dunn, Richard and Mark Senter III, general editors. *Reaching a Generation for Christ.* (Chicago: Moody Press, 1997), 121-138.
2. Warren S. Benson, *Youth Education in the Church* (Chicago: Moody Press, 1978), 9.
3. Howard Gardner, *Frames of Mind: the Theory of Multiple Intelligences* (New York: Basic Books, 1993).
4. Search Institute, "What are the developmental assets?," http://www.search-institute.org/assets, accessed May 2008.
5. Jackson, Allen and Randy Johnson, *Connected, Committed, and a Little Bit Crazy* (Nashville: Convention Press, 1996), 97.

Chapter 4

1. McNabb, Bill and Steven Mabry, *Teaching the Bible Creatively* (Grand Rapids, MI: Zondervan Publishing House, 1990).
2. "Albert Einstein," http://www.brainyquote.com/quotes/quotes/a/alberteins133991.html, accessed April 2008.

IF THEY COME TO YOUR
YOUTH GROUP FOR THE
NEXT SIX YEARS, WHAT
WILL THEY KNOW WHEN
THEY LEAVE?

studentlife**bible**study.com

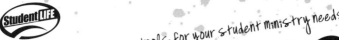